T0345503

# a winter's journey

THE FRENCH LIST

# PAUL VIRILIO

## a winter's journey

FOUR CONVERSATIONS WITH MARIANNE BRAUSCH

TRANSLATED BY CHRIS TURNER

LONDON NEW YORK CALCUTTA

**Seagull Books 2011**

Paul Virilio and Marianne Brausch, *Dialektische Lektionen*: *Vier Gespräche* © Hatje Cantz Verlag, Ostfildern, 1999.

First published in English by Seagull Books, 2011. English translation © Chris Turner

ISBN-13   978 1 9064 9 785 9

**British Library Cataloguing-in-Publication Data**
A catalogue record for this book is available from the British Library

Typeset by Seagull Books, Calcutta, India
Printed and bound by Hyam Enterprises, Calcutta, India

# CONTENTS

Four dialectical interviews between Paul Virilio—aged 64, militant left-wing Christian, urbanist and philosopher of Franco-Italian origin—and Marianne Brausch—disciple of the philosopher, aged 41, of Franco-Luxembourgeois origin, half-Jewish, atheistic, but a believer, in the Old Testament sense, in the 'Word' which is (God). Architect by training, architectural journalist and apprentice writer . . .

'Woman writer,' she says.

'Hold on to your *Sheaffer*,' he says.[1]

1

DIALOGUE BETWEEN MASTER AND PUPIL:
DEATH AND 'THE MAIDEN'
*1940 or the Origins of the Countdown*

*When it began, I*
*was eight years old.*

PAUL VIRILIO. If you like, let's begin by getting into the mood. Have you read the tribute I wrote for Heiner Müller when he died?

MARIANNE BRAUSCH. No . . .

VIRILIO. I'll read it to you because it's a good way of introducing our dialogue between death and 'the maiden'.

Here's the text that I wanted to read at his funeral in Berlin, which was actually read by friends from the *Schaubühne* theatre:

*Heiner Müller, 16 January 1996.*

*I have come to salute my brother. The child of total war and of the totalitarian post-war. The one who saw the storm pass by, the storm that eradicates all peace, beginning with peace of mind. The one who managed to produce his work amid the chaos—work bearing the contradictory stamp of a devastated Europe. A man for whom the end of the world was always a present concern, through the fire and the ruins of the past. My brother of the ashes, who relived the French collapse in the Second World War, Stalingrad, Auschwitz or Berlin, as I lived through the nights of curfew, the splendid horror of the bombing raids, the ruination of cities. On a level with the great tragedians, you proclaimed as a prophet that man is not the centre of the world, but its end, its completion and did so at a time when all the world's misery probably comes from the feeling that man is surpassable, a feeling reinforced by the invention of machines that claim to be his successors. Heiner, my blood brother. Your entire work is there to dispel the fatal illusion of eugenics, that eternal return of the mechanical in its opposition to the animal. With you,*

*friend, a world ends and a world begins, and since*
*to die is to continue to be born, I say A Dieu.*[2]

BRAUSCH. When the philosopher Gilles Deleuze
committed suicide, the newspaper *Libération*, in
its edition of 7 November 1995, published a
passage he had written three years before in his
Afterword to Beckett's *Quad*. Deleuze evoked the
figure of Beckett at the end of his life, 'The
Exhausted One', and wrote: 'Being exhausted is
much more than being tired . . . The tired person
has merely exhausted the doing of some particular thing, whereas the exhausted person exhausts
the whole of the possible . . . Does he exhaust the
possible because he is himself exhausted or is he
exhausted because he has exhausted the possible?
He exhausts himself in exhausting the possible,
and vice versa . . . One was tired of something,
but one is exhausted by nothing.'[3]

VIRILIO. Perfect.

BRAUSCH. In a much simpler, more trivial way,
we can also say that when the birds begin to sing,
war is beginning. And this happens daily—from
time immemorial to the end of the world: the

bird will eat the worm and will itself be eaten . . . and so on. It's war!

VIRILIO. It's war. That will be the subject of this first chapter, '1940 . . .' It turns out that that war was my youth. I was born in 1932. When it began in 1940, I was eight years old. So, it's my university, my father, my mother. I'm going to live from war and in war. I cannot but speak about it because it's my origin. It isn't a choice but a consequence.

BRAUSCH. A matter of fate, like my origins . . .

VIRILIO. An initial fate, an inevitable consequence of birth.

BRAUSCH. What is that beginning?

VIRILIO. First, it's the sudden awareness that war concerns space and time; that it's not just a problem for adults—I'm too young to be aware of the political ins-and-outs; for me, it was space-time that would change violently.

BRAUSCH. You became aware of this or, more exactly, you realized it. And part of your work was subsequently going to be to make others realize it.

VIRILIO. I realize suddenly at the age of eight that the world isn't stable: not only is it unstable, but it's relative. It's relative to technologies—transport or transmission technologies—that are destabilizing and destroying the world.

The problem of war is, first and foremost, a problem of the environment being brought into question; not just the family environment—we moved out of Paris to take refuge in Brittany with my mother's family—but a destabilization of the rhythm of life and the rhythm of relations with others.

It turns out that this war is a war of total mobilization. It isn't just a total war—we'll come back to this—but I have to stress that it's a war of total mobilization. As Ernst Jünger was to say later, it's the machine of total mobilization. Everything's mobilized, not just men in work or at war or in business, but also the very dynamics of relationships, the very dynamics of communications. When we talk of *Blitzkrieg*, of a war of speed, it's clear that this is going to be a source of work for me. But it will be so via events experienced by a child.

*Blitzkrieg* (it's Paul Virilio the adult speaking, but the child Paul Virilio experiences it, senses it, feels it) is, in fact, a war that will call the notion of the border into question. Up to that period, borders were solid: there were troops there, the Maginot Line, the trenches in 1914, the Vauban forts, etc. Now, suddenly, the borders are pierced by the *Panzerdivisionen* and war spreads exactly like a flood.

I often cite this as an example of the sense of being-out-of-phase that I experienced: I'm at Nantes and they tell us on the radio that the German tanks are at Orleans. Suddenly, I hear a noise in the street, run to the window and they're at Nantes! That's *Blitzkrieg*.

BRAUSCH. I can well understand what you mean. I've always lived in Paris, unconsciously or otherwise along the line of the Seine (from conscious choice, I think, rather than from the French origins of part of my family). First literally 'above' it, at the Pont-Neuf, then on the Ile Saint-Louis, and now in the Faubourg St Antoine beyond the place de la Bastille. Every year on 14 July I experience (and I wouldn't miss it for anything in the world) the opposite sensation: I watch the 14 July parade on TV. When I was at the Pont-Neuf, the echo of the passage of the Patrouille de France aerobatic display team in the sky and the actual view of it (since I saw it and always do) were virtually simultaneous. On the Ile Saint-Louis, the two were 30 seconds apart. Now, in the Faubourg, I'm a minute away! But I no longer 'see' the (red, white and blue) trace that *you* saw in the space of aerial warfare—we might say it's vanished into thin air!

VIRILIO. Yes, that total mobilization was, of course, the mobilization of the others, of the British, who were there, and the Germans who were to come. The peoples were intermingled. And then there were the night-time air-raid alerts, the first ones. In other words, foreign planes were flying overhead—something that had never happened before. At school we all had gas masks. We didn't know what a gas mask was and we didn't know what gas warfare was. But quite clearly it produced panic, a sort of collective fear that set in and which bears no relation to individual fear . . .

BRAUSCH. In my family, the story runs that by the end of the war, when the air-raid sirens went, my grandmother would stay rooted to the stairs with her teeth chattering and unable to make it down into the cellar. That's individual fear, I understand what you mean. And since my family was openly (!) Jewish in the Free Zone, they also experienced the 'total' fear of being betrayed to the authorities and then, afterwards, in the Occupied Zone, the collective fear of 'recognition' by the other as a 'secret Jew'. Their false identity cards were very badly forged . . .

VIRILIO. As I see it, that's a very important element. Everyone experiences personal fear; collective fear is of another nature because it involves phantasies, hatreds and racisms—racisms that aren't xenophobic racisms of the kind you speak of in your family's case, but, as I would put it, traditional racisms—which are linked to this collective fear. The fear of the other isn't merely fear of otherness, but fear of the stranger insofar as everyone becomes a stranger. When there's war, you're uncertain of other people's friendship, of the trustworthiness of the person alongside you—is he an informer, etc.? The total mobilization machine means everyone's set in motion; everyone's carried along. It involves logistics or, in other words, the supplying of the troops, the trains running constantly, the roads jammed to bursting, as much as it does ballistics, the deployment of artillery, radio networks, telecommunications. So something new is shaped suddenly: an energy-body. As an example, we might say that the Berlin Olympics already brings this energy-body on to the stage, in the sense that the hero is the one with the greatest energy in his body. And when the black American Jesse Owens beats the handsome Aryan, that spells absolute disgrace for Hitler, who leaves the stadium, because the black man's energy-body is more powerful than the white man's . . .

BRAUSCH. Everything you've said so far, in fact, concerns a change in the notion of temporal rhythm. *Chronos* isn't invariably continuous, even though it flows smoothly . . . in linear fashion, outside us, almost outside the very notion we have of time. Virtually in the animalistic sense, in the sense of the biological clock . . . And suddenly, it speeds up.

VIRILIO. Absolutely. Speed becomes a new rhythm; more exactly, speed becomes a milieu. *Blitzkrieg*—literally, lightning-war (the German term is quite precise, like a flash of lightning in a stormy sky)—is more than the milieu in the territorial or geographical sense: it's the speed milieu. So we can say we've already passed into what I shall describe later as the 'being' of the *traject* (of movement, *Bewegung*). Up to that point, in philosophy, the two 'beings' on which philosophical thinking is based are the object and the subject. The object and the subject—in the sense of objectivity and subjectivity. Yet, we've forgotten a third term, which is the *traject* and trajectivity. During the Second World War we experienced trajectivity: through the assault of the Panzer tanks, through the war of the airwaves—the radio—quite obviously through the bombs and the rockets that would make their appearance (the V1s and V2s were the first manifestations) and through radar.

BRAUSCH. A suddenly invisible traject with the 'real' appearance of the un-real . . .

VIRILIO. Quite. We're already in a world that presages everything that's going to follow in the post-war period, and even in the Modernity of this century's end. We'll see this later.

One of the things that marked me, then (since this first interview is about my childhood memories during the Occupation), was the idea that the sky had been invaded in the same way as the land. That was without parallel—an unprecedented event for my generation. In those days aviation was an exceptional thing: there were no airlines, there were practically no planes in the sky. It was, in fact, something of the order of play, like beach games in the 1950s and '60s. Planes made advertising flights, sky-writing round the Eiffel Tower and the like. But there was no such thing as air traffic. It was the war that brought these great squadrons of bombers that would invade the sky and turn Fortress Europe into a roofless fortress.

BRAUSCH. As we've said, that overturned the order of time and rhythm, overturned horizontality and the horizontal world. We were seeing the birth of vertical space . . .

VIRILIO. Yes, and the third dimension. The war took place in the third dimension of space, not just in the two dimensions of the army and the navy. From now on, we'd have an air war and a strategy of aerial destruction; and that would be the way of it until the destruction of Hiroshima, which marked the tragic last word—the 'end'— of the war.

There was in the sky what at the time were called 'atmosphere machines'. This is a term that was picked up by Céline.[4] It's connected with the vapour trails from those thousands of bombers in the sky which greatly astonished us. It's a term that well expresses our anxiety at this occupied sky. It's at this point we understand that war is total, because it 'exists' in the sky.

BRAUSCH. You spoke a moment ago of 'this roofless world', which is, as I too see it, an extraordinary image to express the idea that space is occupied or—more precisely—occupiable! The plane has passed, yet its trace remains. And you see it in this roofless world.

VIRILIO. Exactly. And what's also extraordinary is that, with this, we're in a double bind. That is to say that, on the ground, we're with our enemies and our allies are in the sky. Space is very quickly liberated because of Allied air supremacy. So we regard the sky both as the source of death—as is well known, Allied bombers made 'mistakes' and also cruel but necessary decisions to bury 'us' beneath the bombs intended for the Germans—and as a source of liberatory hope. It's terrifying for a child to be torn like this between two situations.

BRAUSCH. This is your experience of being torn—
an experience that must also have left many
adults feeling equally torn. Not to mention the
entire Allied camp!

VIRILIO. Yes, definitely. But I believe the terror
was magnified for the child that I was then—a
child who, I say again, was just discovering life
in those conditions! Can you imagine it . . . an
atmosphere laden with both death and freedom!

BRAUSCH. Yes, what a terrible conflict.

VIRILIO. As I said in *L'Insécurité du Territoire*,[5] I
was like Nero, because I'd chosen which side I
was on. I was delighted for my city, Nantes, to be
destroyed—8,000 buildings were destroyed—I
was delighted, while at the same time being afraid
of the death and destruction involved . . . I was
Nero, happy to see Rome burn!

BRAUSCH. Death is liberation—we're back with
Müller, whom you have now commended to
God by bidding him 'A Dieu' . . . It's true, that
was a terrifying liberation.

VIRILIO. A liberation by death, yes. But which was
to free us from the Occupation to go back to the

'real' of that time. We came back to the notion of space-time.

BRAUSCH. Life and death or horizontal occupation and vertical liberation . . .

VIRILIO. Horizontal occupation, but vertical liberation . . . I remember that at the time that sky was a sky from which there also came information. Leaflets were dropped from planes informing us about what was going on. And we children ran through the fields and streets to pick them up, to read the news falling from the heavens.

BRAUSCH. What poetry! A devilish, hellish beauty! And, if we make a more trivial comparison, what a sudden discrepancy between the ear glued to the coded radio messages—'Ici Londres'—and the sudden direct news literally falling out of the sky!

VIRILIO. It was a significant, utopian event, since, it must be said, we were living in a utopia. World war is a utopia. Nothing is stable any more. For children, that goes way beyond any reality.

And here's another element/event that's always coming to mind, a second perception I have of the war. I'm in Nantes in 1943 with my mother. I'm eleven years old. We're queuing up at the biscuit factory to get LU biscuits for the prisoners of war and, to give me a break, my mother sends me off to the rue du Calvaire (Calvary Street!) where all the big toyshops are. She wants me to 'get a bit of air', as it were. And what a lot of 'air' I get, since the street has been bombed by the Allies that very afternoon and has disappeared! Disappeared, vanished, literally gone up in smoke.

BRAUSCH. Blown away. In the name of 'taking some air' . . . What a paradox again! Everything is 'in the air'. Where once there was a city, there's nothing. Nantes wasn't a real city, then, but a Potemkin city?[6]

VIRILIO. Yes, the entire centre of Nantes was razed to the ground. When we go back there in the smoke and the horror of the bombing, we can see the horizon in the distance. In other words, for me the city is just stage scenery: it can be whisked away, as you've just said. In an instant the real city becomes a Potemkin city. For a child, a city is a solid thing; it's like the Alps, it's eternal.

Something like that can't be reduced to ruins. But in this case it took just an hour's bombing and the city was gone.

BRAUSCH. That puts me in mind of a bit of documentary film Wim Wenders used—I think it's in *Wings of Desire*—where you see a building that's had its facade blown away, and in this hollowed-out building there's a woman shaking a red eiderdown as if through a window, but she's simply shaking it in the void. The window frame has gone and there's nothing standing. I was very much affected by that.

VIRILIO. I can attest here to something I actually saw. I remember a house that had lost its facade and I saw an old man in his bedroom. We went to wake him up because he'd heard nothing . . .

BRAUSCH. That may sound like a humorous anecdote, but it's tragic!

I'm going to jump forward here—we'll come back to this since he was your friend and it was indeed you who started him writing—I'm thinking of Georges Perec who, throughout his life—his whole life long—'exhausted' places. What was he looking for, that lost child of the war? What was he seeking, if not himself through the excavation of the real, since he had nothing solid to hang on to, no family any more? When I read in *Je suis né*[7] (that fantastic title for a writer who can at last say 'I') . . . when I read in that tiny book the distinction he makes between 'native land' and 'promised land', I have each time a memory—a collective memory—of my origins, a memory that's in me and that both hurts me and makes me— painfully—jubilant at one and the same time. I'm Nero too. I've chosen which side I'm on.

But I wanted particularly to mention here *Life: A User's Manual*, in which he lifts the facade on a Haussmannian block in Paris and shows us the lives going on in the various apartments like a jigsaw puzzle.[8] A puzzle in which, at the end, through the story of the novel—since the connecting thread is, after all, a novel taking place in the building—everything fits together, thanks to the finding of the last piece. Perec, 'the man with the scar', to whom Jean Duvignaud pays tribute—

as he pays tribute also to you who walked with him in Paris—had in the end found himself, thanks to his work which you so aptly termed 'infra-ordinary' . . .[9] His experience is different from yours, but he's your brother 'in shock(s)'! And you too found yourself through these childhood shocks. To the point of also making your life's work out of them. It's extraordinary! I envy you the 'gloomy spirits' that came of that! But it's well known that they prompted quite a lot of people to write, to create their world, a world, the world.

VIRILIO. We'll have an opportunity to speak of that. At length! But let's come back to our initial premises, my initial premises. This idea that suddenly the city all around me is ultimately just scenery was to profoundly modify my relation to the real and my relationship with others. From that point on, I'd become a relativist.

BRAUSCH. The adult within the child is born. He gets some distance from the world. Excuse me for quoting myself again, but our 'contract' is for a dialogue (you hit the nail on the head in speaking of 'death and the maiden', with which I identify myself in this chapter): I too became an adult—though this is something you didn't know—and a relativist too on the night, when I was eleven, following the day (an Easter day, a day of Resurrection!) . . . when my father died. Who is a child's prop if not her father?

VIRILIO. I go further. I become relativistic, that is to say, literally, that I shall no longer believe my eyes. But I understand your terrible doubt on the day of the Resurrection. For my part, I become a conscientious objector.

BRAUSCH. You go more quickly at any rate! I'm a bit like Perec, I had a wound that kept me suspended between native land and promised land . . .

VIRILIO. Yes, perhaps I was able to relativize more quickly! I'd remind you that the first form of conscientious objection is no longer believing one's eyes. Having doubts about what you see. It doesn't just mean refusing to do your military service, as they say. Conscientious objection is when there's a hiatus between real perception—one's eyes—and the conception of the real. One doesn't simply perceive the real through one's eyes, but through a delayed process of thought. That is to say, you have doubts about the real. From that moment on, I had doubts about the real.

BRAUSCH. From the time my father died, I've had doubts about the real. My conscientious objection consisted in ceasing to believe in my religion: dying on the symbolic day of Christ's Resurrection . . . But you reconcile me a little with this initial wound, as you did with Perec. 'Adieu, à Dieu' you say to Müller . . .

VIRILIO. I cast doubt on the real. Not only in the obvious sense of asking, when I see a man or woman: 'Is this a friend or an enemy, an informer?—there's plenty of them'. But in addition to casting doubt on the real, I no longer believe in the reality of the world.

Quite obviously, this all goes together with an extraordinary degree of propaganda that's unimaginable to us today. To attempt to imagine it, we can perhaps make a comparison with the Gulf War (we'll come back to this later). But the propaganda during the Second World War was very different in nature from TV propaganda, since it came to us through the radio and the cinema. The newsreels in particular.

BRAUSCH. Marc Ferro is working on this, showing us the truths and counter-truths of the two sides in his programme *Histoires parallèles* on the Franco-German channel 'Arte' . . .

VIRILIO. Yes, the newsreels were the TV of the day. But sometimes we were eight days behind with what was happening in Russia, in Libya with Rommel, the destroyed cities, etc. That is to say, we were totally 'radio-controlled'. On the one hand by Radio London . . .

BRAUSCH. And 'cinema-controlled' . . .

VIRILIO. As you mentioned earlier, by the propaganda films, of course, which were fed to us by the *Propagandastaffel*.

BRAUSCH. It was the *Propagandastaffel* that more or less gave filmed news its first run-out . . .

VIRILIO. Absolutely. And I wrote the book *War and Cinema* later, but it goes without saying that first I lived it.[10] These films were remarkably well made, as can be seen in *Histoires parallèles*. So I experienced that 'live', and it's clear that reality became a montage of the events. I'm not talking any longer of the city as stage-scenery here, of the uncertainty about the people I'm alongside, but about the montage, the editing of the events.

BRAUSCH. This is how you, Paul Virilio, were born: and you know how to decipher messages, thanks to your early experience of conscientious objection!

VIRILIO. Yes. I saw the so-called Red Poster for the 'Armenians'—a resistance group led by the Armenian Missak Manouchian, whom the Nazis presented as a common criminal. I saw it at Nantes. I was twelve years old when I saw the poster for the Armenians who were shot. We were 'snared'—and this is something that makes me entirely opposed and resistant to cybernetics, 'cyberspace' and advertising today—snared by that 'advertising', which was remarkably well constructed. A magazine like *Signal*, of which I still have some copies, was outstandingly well put together, as were the German newsreels . . .

BRAUSCH. I'm going to interrupt you here. I've always asked my mother why my grandfather—who was an intelligent man—hadn't sent his daughters to America in '38 or '39. My family left, you see, during the *Débâcle*, on the morning of 10 May 1940, and drove to the south of France, into the *Zone libre*! He was, as I now understand, completely misinformed. But he thought the Maginot Line was a reality: 'We're going to hang out the washing on the Siegfried Line . . .'

VIRILIO. Exactly. This is a good illustration of what I'm saying. In order to know what was going on, you had to not believe your eyes any more! You had to build up a reality through the radio from London, through information spread by the Resistance (there were little news-sheets and leaflets) and through the films we went to see. We had to have some entertainment, after all, and we went to the pictures. That went on for a full five years . . .

We were in a system of a war of the airwaves, a phenomenon of 'fictional montage' that was extraordinarily effective, I'd say, because, even if

I no longer believed my eyes, I was only ten or twelve years old at the time!

BRAUSCH. . . . and what came over the airwaves was radically different, depending on whether it came from the German or the Allied side. It isn't easy to construct one's own religion—I say this with Jewish humour—but, in leaving on 10 May 1940, my family, which 'believed' in what it 'saw', also partly went up in smoke itself . . . Today we know that some believed in the 'delousing' story right to the doors of the gas chambers. So . . .

VIRILIO. . . . Yes, it's tragic. But that's also linked to human nature, to the hope of 'Everyone'. However, we have to dis-hope!

So, to go on, the sky belonged to the Allies, the land to the Germans, the radio to the Allies and the cinema to the Germans! We got no pictures from London, we only got sounds.

BRAUSCH. The invention of a real lie! Diabolical and schizophrenic!

VIRILIO. Yes, quite. And a collective fear went with this sense of 'unhooking' from reality.

BRAUSCH. I'd say the sense of reality being un-hinged . . .

VIRILIO. You weren't sure of reality. And not just of the stability of the city, which could be devas-tated in a single bombing raid, but also of the friendship of your friends or the love of your lovers, who betrayed you and informed on you. This was a situation that was traumatic for me; not a birth trauma, but a childhood trauma.

BRAUSCH. Perhaps I'm being stubborn about this, but it was still a kind of birth, since you became aware of how the world functions 'naturally' and how it is—artificially—manipulated. And if you hadn't lived through these events as a child, been a victim of them and become aware of them, you wouldn't be the philosopher and writer Paul Virilio!

VIRILIO. Yes, and it is indeed then that I begin to write.

BRAUSCH. You see!

VIRILIO. I take a notebook and make it 'my' note-book—though I've never found it again since—

called *Five Years of War* . . . I'll finish it in 1945 at the Liberation . . . and I relate my experience. Because I want, like Kafka, to write in an effort to understand.

BRAUSCH. Like Perec, who 'exhausts places' in an effort to understand . . . And like me talking here to you . . .

VIRILIO. I write with lots of spelling mistakes, not to mention stylistic errors, but I'm only a kid, and when you're ten or twelve, you're not that brilliant at writing, particularly when you haven't done much literary study in those years! And I remember that 'radio control' made a lot of things possible. As De Gaulle said, 'without Radio London, I wouldn't have existed'; Hitler too wouldn't have had the power he had without the radiotelephone, which enabled him to tell Rommel what to do or to tell von Paulus not to surrender at Stalingrad! So, it's both good and bad.

BRAUSCH. Yes, good and evil! That's where the importance of technical devices shows itself— and of the logistical support they bring into play.

VIRILIO. Quite. Everything revolves around the technical devices . . .

BRAUSCH. . . . which, later—we'll come back to this—become hyper-dangerous, since a device that's also invented at that time is the atom bomb, with which, as you've said, the 'end' to the war will be written, an end that bears the names Hiroshima and Nagasaki, then morphs into a threat during the Cold War and leads us perhaps to an ecological reaction today . . . ? I don't really know what to call it, but it's a deliquescence— perhaps, I'll clarify this—a perversion where the eco-urban architecture of the 1990s is concerned, which is perhaps merely consolation through a camouflaging of the elements inherent in the construction of architecture.

VIRILIO. At any rate, it's certain that there's a split personality there. For me, technology is both the best and the worst. And I've always believed this. In a way, then, this split is a phenomenon that will develop during the totalitarian post-war period— I stress that, if the war was total, the post-war period was totalitarian—and we've been part of it.

Not just the communists and not just the surviving fascists, but we too. We as citizens and as architects and urbanists have simply been participants in it, like it or not. We'll have a chance to talk about this when we come to urban utopias.

BRAUSCH. Yes, let's get back to our dear old technical devices!

VIRILIO. The war of the airwaves also involved an extraordinary device that we first heard talk of at that time. I'm referring to radar. Radar was extraordinary. Why? Because it was the beginning of remote control. That is to say, you could 'touch' things at a distance. Obviously you don't touch them with your hand, but with a wave that will rebound off a plane or a ship: you know it's 'there', without seeing it, by radar echo. This was an unprecedented thing for us, a fantasy object. Touching an object by way of waves is something that had never been seen before! And there it was, radar. Like the first rockets, the V1s and V2s. And the Germans made a big thing of their rockets, since these 'weapons of revenge' were going to be the weapons that would enable them to win the war.

Radar is interesting because it underpins the idea of this cybernetic space. It's already in a world of the invisible, of presence, of tactility, of tele-tactility across the airwaves.

BRAUSCH. It's the invention of the virtual utilization of space.

VIRILIO. It's just that. It's the beginning of remote control. I remember that, on the landing beaches, the Germans were to put little Goliath tanks that were 2 or 3 metres long and a metre wide. They were tiny, but were called 'Goliaths'! After all, the Germans couldn't call them 'Davids'!

BRAUSCH. You make me laugh, but that's so horribly true!

VIRILIO. Yes, but let's be serious again. What were they? They were tanks that were remote-controlled from bunkers and advanced on the enemy. This was, in fact, a charge in the classical sense. They were remote-controlled by a cable—we would call this 'wire-guidance' now—and they exploded, blowing up the Allied tanks as they landed. That happened in 1944. And there was also the remote control of the first B17s. Just at the time of the Liberation, we would see the first film of B17 bombers taking off without pilots. There's a camera inside—one of the first video cameras—and you see the plane taking off. There's no one in the plane, but someone on the ground, in a sort of look-out post, is flying the plane.

BRAUSCH. Like children today who play with remote-controlled cars in the town squares . . .

VIRILIO. Except that here we're talking about a big plane! We're getting into a world that will be underwritten by Wiener—I'll remind you that it was Norbert Wiener who theorized the nascent discipline of cybernetics in 1945–47, drawing on Claude E. Shannon's information theory, and publicized the 'electronic turtle' automata, which already had a degree of intelligence. We can see that the war of the airwaves, as you so well put it, introduces us to a virtuality that terrorizes us because . . .

BRAUSCH. A real virtuality! . . .

VIRILIO. Yes, real! . . . Because it has an effect on the world—an effect of both destruction and liberation. From all that we've said here, there are, of course, other elements that emerge. But first there's the landscape of war. The landscape of war isn't just a landscape like any other.

A few years ago I gave a lecture on 'the landscape of war' at the École du paysage in Versailles. It was a great success, not because I said what I had to say particularly well but because they had never heard anything about this.

BRAUSCH. Nor had I.

VIRILIO. With Bosnia, with what's happening with current wars, we're beginning to understand.

You'll see, the war landscape is a landscape of events. In other words, the landscape is no longer simply a thing of relief, of trees and hills, etc. It's made up of explosions, shockwaves, craters that are constantly changing it . . . it's a thing of sound and fury, of vaporization, of smoke . . .

BRAUSCH. The use of gas at Ypres in 1914 provided a sort of testing ground . . .

VIRILIO. . . . . a thing of vibrations and, I would say, it involves a sense of the destruction of space—not simply of land or houses but also of space. When you're being bombed, as I often was, you have the impression that what's being destroyed isn't just the houses around you but reality itself, with the disappearance of your body next on the agenda . . .

BRAUSCH. . . . .What happened at Hiroshima was an inverted volcanic eruption.

VIRILIO. Absolutely. So, it's a landscape. Which means that you can love it. And remember that line of Apollinaire's: *Ah Dieu, que la guerre est jolie*![11] Yes, you can say that when you've been under bombardment. You can't say it when you're just a witness to war.

BRAUSCH. No. Otherwise, it's perverse. But I can well understand what you're saying. It's shocking, but you understand it if you also see it as: 'I got out of there alive'!

VIRILIO. Yes. When you've been a victim of war, as I was as a kid, you can say, '*Ah Dieu, que la guerre est jolie!*'

BRAUSCH. As a headstrong, intrepid adolescent, my aunt went swimming in the river Creuse— braving the curfew, by the way—and brought back fragments of the bombs, still warm, to my terrified grandfather. And, again in lethal danger on account of the curfew, she sat on her balcony at night, watching the bombing, and saw the bombs and tracer flares going off like fireworks!

VIRILIO. Yes! That kind of horror's a magnificent spectacle. When you're in a night-time air raid, the tracer-bullets, the searchlights and the explosions make for an extraordinary 'light show'! As you say, there's a perversion of taste that makes us enjoy horror. Some people have taken this love of horror to the extreme, to the point of becoming horrible people through inflicting death on others. But then there are all those who, like me, were spectators. Not TV spectators, as in the (first) Gulf War, but spectators of the beauty of horror. The war landscape has haunted me since.

BRAUSCH. And it's truly perverse—though I come back to the 'attenuation' I mentioned just now!

VIRILIO. It's all perverse. Nothing's pure, because it's the threat of death—or simply death itself—that's at the end of your aunt's balcony, as she watches the show: 'Oh, what a nice blue, what a lovely red! . . .'

But the war landscape is something else too. It's going to have an impact on the normal landscape. That landscape becomes camouflage. Everything will be camouflaged and that's extraordinary . . .

BRAUSCH. That's perverse again. That must give a delightful sense of power—and of security too. But mingled with fear.

VIRILIO. Camouflage means blackout . . . You can't open the curtains any more, you can't switch the lights on when night falls. Car head-lamps are blue . . .

BRAUSCH. That's so far as the civilians are concerned, the 'passive warfare' of the civilian populations, for whom passive resistance is something they undergo. What about 'active warfare' and the enemy?

VIRILIO. That's right. As we'll see, 'active warfare', 'active camouflage' as you might say, was used by both the Allies and the Germans. On the enemy side, on the ground, shapes are modified with nets and branches. The colours change: everything is khaki. And here we come to Allied camouflage: the Allied planes were painted blue underneath and green on top. This means that when the enemy was above them they merged into the ground, and seen from the ground they merged into the sky.

BRAUSCH. It's 'the world turned upside down'. Just listening to you I almost feel dizzy, as if I'm on a roller coaster at the funfair! And what a roller coaster it was! And then this inversion of sky and earth is another perversity: it's an inversion of space.

VIRILIO. Quite. It was also, already, the aesthetics of disappearance.

BRAUSCH. Excuse me, but I make a connection with contemporary architecture here, with the architecture of the 1990s, the work of the youngest architects which isn't far removed from 'land art' and, as you say, from camouflage. When they 'clothe' their buildings in natural elements, they're camouflaging them . . . This is what I call eco-urban architecture.

VIRILIO. Yes, that's a good point. And there was already, at the time, an aesthetics of the disappearance of everything we've just mentioned. In other words, the things are there but they're concealed. Here again, you couldn't trust what you saw. You thought you saw a tank, for example, but in fact it was an inflatable tank that had been placed at a particular location. The Allies did this all along the southern coast of England—inflatable planes too . . .

BRAUSCH. I didn't know that. But that's another perversion, since I take it that it was to make the enemy believe they had more resources than they really had. To come back to what you just said about a roofless Fortress Europe, this was a faked-up Fortress Great Britain! Vauban[12] in plastic— extraordinary!

VIRILIO. Moreover, it was a strategic deception, since it was done to make the Germans think the Allies would land in the Pas-de-Calais area whereas they were preparing to land in Normandy.

BRAUSCH. These are, in fact, modern resources being deployed but for the purposes of classical warfare . . . this was a Potemkin army!

VIRILIO. That's right.

BRAUSCH. The way we have balloons today that are heart-shaped or shaped like Mickey Mouse . . .

VIRILIO. Yes, though in this case, they were in-flatable balloons shaped like planes or tanks. It was a perversion, whereas what you're talking about is of the order of play.

BRAUSCH. Yes, but as you said yourself a moment ago, '*Ah que la guerre est jolie!*'

VIRILIO. I admit it . . . But let's get back to the 'real virtuality' of camouflage, since this camou-flage will impact on absolutely everything.

And we're coming to one of the important subjects that concerns both of us in our 'civilian'

professions today, which is—let's not forget—
one of the main themes of this book . . .

BRAUSCH. Architecture. Up to today's eco-urban
architecture, which is no longer an architecture
of transparency, as in the 1980s (was that, I ask
myself, a democratic state of grace or a delusion?),
but an architecture of disappearance. We well
know, given the difficulties of current society and
of the architectural profession itself in this mael-
strom, that it's war once again. Architects are, as
it were, 'paralysed', 'rooted to the spot' by a task
that seems insurmountable because of develop-
ments which are beyond them and which they
don't understand—sadly, even more radically
than the way you as a child didn't understand
war, though indeed it is war. Except perhaps these
attempts at camouflage by the young 'eco-urbans'
of the 1990s . . .

VIRILIO. Yes, but we're still only at basic premises
here. And the basic premise is the bunker. Bunker
architecture is an aero-static architecture. That's
to say, it's an architecture that must let projectiles

slide off it, not stop them with sharp edges. Hence, its forms are rounded, partly so that you see them less within the site—I'd remind you that organic forms are round forms.

BRAUSCH. Yes, there are no edges, nothing to stop anything . . . like the morphological forms of nature which everything slides off too—the rain, the wind . . .

VIRILIO. So that architecture's already anthropomorphic or zoomorphic. More precisely, I'd say geomorphic. And what you've just said about today's architecture is very true: it's the same. But let's get back to the argument. You have three spaces, then, that give rise to each other. We've spoken about the military space with regard to aerialization. As Malevich said, the world becomes aerial, it aerializes. So the military space, from now on, is aerial, unlike the 1914–18 War, which was the last classical war where the handling of men, of infantry, was concerned. The country becomes a fortress with bunkers all along the coast. We have this with Fortress Europe, the

Maginot Line, the Siegfried Line and the Atlantic Wall. And all this is based on the monolith or, in other words, on an object that isn't grounded in the earth but centred in itself and capable of resisting the tremors to which the terrain is subjected; it's a bit like a stone or a pebble on the sand, which is self-stabilizing.

I'll give you an example of madness where military space is concerned: I'm thinking of Goering travelling between Berlin and Carinhall, his villa outside the capital. Since he very often drove from Berlin, where he worked at Luftwaffe HQ, to his residence, to enjoy the masterpieces he'd looted from all over Europe, he knew—as they were aware of his habits—that he'd be attacked en route by Allied planes. Rommel was killed that way, on the road, in an Allied air attack.

What did he do? Since he knew there was a chance he'd be attacked from the sky, which was already under enemy control, he calculated the time it would take to stop the car and take refuge in a bunker. And all along the road, he built evenly spaced bunkers so that he could stop on his journey and shelter from the bombs.

BRAUSCH. We come back to movement and space-time!

VIRILIO. Quite. What began with *Blitzkrieg* ends with the *Bunker*, the monolith: Hitler's bunker, Goering's bunkers. It's extraordinary!

BRAUSCH. He didn't think of digging a tunnel? Was it too far? Otherwise, the lightning war would have ended the way the phoney war—the time when Sartre was peacefully writing his *War Diaries*—began, with the two sides observing each other from a static position in the trenches. Or at Verdun . . . it was ever thus. Compare the catacombs of the first Christians in Rome: it was either martyrdom in the arena from wild beasts—that was war—or the catacombs . . . Or quite simply a cat-and-mouse game, if I can put it that way, like the Resistance fighters out in the field . . .

VIRILIO. No, it was too far for a tunnel. But, having said that, they did that with factories. Most factories were buried underground. Think of the tunnel at the Dora camp, where the slave workers worked on the V2s . . . Lots of German factories were built beneath the Harz forest. So there was a kind of 'burial' . . .

BRAUSCH. A word that carries a premonitory sense of self-inflicted death. Because they knew, after all, that it was the end. Otherwise they wouldn't have buried themselves to try and produce their last-ditch instruments of death!

VIRILIO. Absolutely . . . German productive power was buried, then, in an attempt to resist air domination, to resist domination of the aerial military space.

But, let's come back to Paul Virilio as a child. Of course, I experienced shelters and cellars. I experienced that fear of the bombings and very soon after the war I would be very sensitive to this kind of protection: my mind had been alerted to it; I knew very early on what *Lebensraum* was.

BRAUSCH. The 'bubble' as they say in ergonomics. Moreover, we don't like it when others enter our bubble . . .

VIRILIO. Yes. And Hitler said, 'The idea of protection haunts and fills our lives,' which clearly shows that living space was a space of fear. This *Lebensraum* wasn't a space of life but a space of the fear of death, a fear Nazism attempted to extend to the whole of the population. And not just to the German population but, of course, to the populations they intended to dominate, exterminate or win over to the 'thousand-year Third Reich'.

BRAUSCH. Can we say too in a positive way that, by dint of this fear, this becomes a survival space?

VIRILIO. Of course. Quite. The bunker isn't Le Corbusier's 'machine for living', but a machine for surviving. Shelters or bunkers of whatever kind are machines for surviving. They're the antithesis of Le Corbusier's 'machine for living'.

BRAUSCH. Which I would myself almost call a machine for 'over-living', in the sense in which we speak of overdrive with an engine. In this case, we'd be talking about an excessiveness of life. I've never liked Le Corbusier's urban theories because of this 'forced' side—like a plant that's been forced with fertilizer. He forces us to live beyond our means.

VIRILIO. That's your interpretation and we'll come back to it. To get back to the earlier argument, this is why, where bunkers are concerned, I talk of crypts.

And there are three myths in architectonic symbolics: the myth of the arch, which bridges and with which you can bind things together; of the nave—the *duomo*—the nave of a church is an inverted ship's hull; and of the church crypt, the crypt of the dead or the crypt of war, the bunker.

BRAUSCH. The arch is also the triumphal arch, beneath which the conqueror makes the defeated soldiers parade, in order to humiliate them . . .

VIRILIO. And the Arc de Triomphe in Paris, where the unknown soldier is buried . . . a place for prayer.

When the end of the war arrived—we're in 1945 now and I'm an hour away from St Nazaire by railcar and I'd never seen the sea—as soon as the Liberation came, I dashed off to go and see the ocean. The discovery of the sea was a wonderful thing. It was an element unknown to me!

BRAUSCH. It's the infinite horizon which, opening the little boy's eyes, suddenly, in its infinite liberation, encapsulates and concentrates all he has lived through and enables him to understand it consciously . . .

VIRILIO. I was thirteen years old. I describe discovering the sea, when I went down to La Baule, in *Bunker Archaeology*.[13] And what did I see when I arrived? The infinity you speak of, because the beach at La Baule is very large. And what did I see on that great expanse of sand: a bunker. What was it? It looked like a German helmet . . . it was a shock discovery.

BRAUSCH. This shock, the bunker—similar to the human skull and hence to the helmet—will bring you much later, when we talk about the Internet, to the analogy with the 'Call Room' (*chambre d'appel*) 'virtual vestibule' and, at the other end of the scale, the 'Urban Beacon' (*balise urbaine*) 'survivor station' for the homeless.

VIRILIO. So, after the war, of course, much later in 1957 (because, after all this, we have to jump forward a bit), the post-war period had arrived and I found myself standing at the foot of a bunker and curious about that architecture, because I had the impression it would provide me with the key to total war. I knew there were bunkers everywhere and that, if I could get a handle on these objects, I was going to understand, to put down some markers . . .

BRAUSCH. The word you use there, *baliser*, is perfect since it means normally to mark out and so on, but also, in slang, it indicates an undefined fear. It's like the way young people today, in the insecure conditions of the inner cities, with unemployment, violence, theft and drugs—in short, all these consequences of inactivity in a 'lost' society in which they find no place for themselves—speak of feeling 'aggro' but not of what they feel 'aggro' about. They hate everything, but don't know what it is they hate . . .

VIRILIO. Absolutely. I was now going to 'mark out' (*baliser*)—consciously—this abstract space that I experienced as a child and that frightened me. So, for ten years I was going to be searching, as an archaeologist. All along the Atlantic Wall, in Germany and all over the place. I'd plot layouts, buy maps to track aerial photographs, etc. It would be a labour of initiation into total warfare.

BRAUSCH. By demystifying it!

VIRILIO. Yes, I opened my eyes and what struck me at the time was the difference from modern architecture. Apart from Le Corbusier, whom I got to know when Ronchamp was being built . . .[14]

BRAUSCH. That just had to be: Le Corbusier, the sculptor of Ronchamp, and Paul Virilio, the archaeologist of the anthropomorphic forms of bunkers . . .

VIRILIO. . . . and the influence on Le Corbusier of the submarine base of La Pallice, when he was working in Chandigarh. The government palace in Chandigarh is inspired by the submarine base at La Pallice! He even wrote about this. He even made a plan for restructuring La Rochelle-La Pallice along the lines of the La Pallice submarine base.

BRAUSCH. Why? What did he find so interesting in it?

VIRILIO. Like me, he thought it was interesting architecturally.

And, to come back to myself, I was discovering modern architecture and bunker architecture, which went together. It was an architecture of a quite other kind than that of seaside villas or of Reconstruction, etc. I discovered an interest in it and I still think that military buildings have a quality which, sadly, civilian ones don't always match. That's why I nuance my judgement by comparison with yours where this sur-vival as *over*-living is concerned, insofar as you find an exaggerated variant of Le Corbusier's 'machines for living' in it.

BRAUSCH. All right.

VIRILIO. So I'll have a long labour of taking photos, drawing plans of layouts, etc., before me.

BRAUSCH. You're totally at one with yourself: *balisage*, the marking of territory, fractals—you're ahead of Mandelbrot's linear fractals! In short, the mapping out of linear territory, 'bounded' by bunkers . . .

VIRILIO. That was exactly what I was going to do. I walked miles and miles of coastline. It took me ten years. At the time I knew nothing of architecture, but *that* architecture fascinated me.

It fascinated me because—apart from the painting I was doing at the time, which we'll speak of in Interview 2—I was interested in a sculptor who'd lived through the war, Henry Moore. He made drawings in the tunnels of the London Underground during the air raids, which inspired his sculptures: recumbent women with holes in them. And bunkers, for me, had something to do with this opening in the middle 'à la Moore'.

BRAUSCH. 'À la Moore' sounds nice . . . It sounds like 'A l'amour'—'to the love of women', to the resurrection of life . . . But we also know the interest Moore had in skulls—in death (*à la mort*).

VIRILIO. 'À la Moore' it is! Because it's true that, without 'à la Moore', without *l'amour*, in the sense of the interest I had at the time in bunkers,

I'd never have come to architecture and urbanism. Never. The work I was doing at the time on military space, I was doing both on real and virtual space, on the solid city and the city as mere backdrop, on the perverse relation to the Other, on the perverse relation to the landscape, since the landscape is faked and camouflaged, as are human beings, sounds and light . . . The bunker is a kind of boundary marker that would enable me to 'get at' total warfare.

BRAUSCH. Yes. It's also, as I suggested above, your 'rescue beacon' (*balise de sauvetage*) today in a city that has no markers; it's the solid element you found that enables you to hang on to reality and to disencrypt—through this 'crypt', as you put it just now—the experience and traumas of the child. Things stop spinning and you can analyze the *Blitzkrieg*.

VIRILIO. That's just the right expression. And, in fact, Hitler never visited the Atlantic Wall because he was aware it was his failure. There was the war of movement, general mobilization, the *Blitzkrieg*.

But once he came to the water . . . he couldn't go any further than the monoliths.

BRAUSCH. Whereas the space and the horizon that the Allies—and Allied movement—came from was open and made counter-mobility possible. The Germans had lost the war.

VIRILIO. That's right. We have here an object that marks the culmination of total war at the foot of—on the threshold of—the liquid continent, the hydrosphere—in other words, of another element where the Anglo-Saxons were in control. And this marked a new stage in their historic conquest of the sea. If the Europeans have been masters of the land since the Romans, the Anglo-Saxons have been masters of the sea and air, given that, at the time, they had the superior air and sea power.

BRAUSCH. But sea and sky are the same thing: the space of liberation, free space in which it's easy to move around.

VIRILIO. And, with the bunker, I found a fixed point, a point I could measure and analyze and that enabled me to extrapolate from, and analyze, my experience.

BRAUSCH. An experience . . . you slough off and on which later you'll build the *balise urbaine* project for the homeless, which will be controversial and will lead to physical attacks, threats and your being publicly denounced once again. Yet you were so right. It would be so useful as a survival tool in today's society . . . Perhaps people will understand better now . . . if they read this book?

VIRILIO. Yes . . . that upset me a lot, even hurt me. But let's come back to the period we were talking about, when I wasn't simply 'de-mystifying', as you put it. Since it was from that starting point, from the starting point of Europe at war, that I set about discovering geostrategy and geopolitics . . .

And it must be said here—because this will bring us on to other terrain later—it was at the same moment that we discovered the existence of the concentration camps. It was at the end of the war, like everyone else, of course, that I discovered the camps. I never thought about that during the war.

BRAUSCH. I know. I spoke about them with my family. When they were refugees in the *Zone libre*, they didn't know yet. There was just the threat of people betraying you to the authorities . . . But we know today that the Allies knew, that the British knew and the Americans too . . . But that's another story . . .

VIRILIO. I wasn't told about it. As you say, it wasn't something 'people' talked about. There were the men who were executed, the hostages, the prisoners—I knew about that, I lived through that. But 'people' didn't know about the camps. We found out only at the end of the war. And, there again, it was an unthinkable, unplaceable thing for a child. You wouldn't believe it. Once again, I didn't believe my eyes, until I saw the first concentration camp survivors getting off the trains . . .

BRAUSCH. And we know, though only now, that Auschwitz, for example, was architecture, real architecture, a purpose-built town, built as a 'labour camp', a perverse town built by architects!

VIRILIO. Yes, it's terrible. It's the ideal city turned upside down. It's a reverse, perverse Fourierism . . .

BRAUSCH. . . . which the Holocaust-deniers deny and, hence, render unreal. It's the persistence of perversity still.

VIRILIO. The Holocaust-deniers camouflage reality perversely; by way of History. But camouflaging is what they are doing.

BRAUSCH. Yes, it's exactly that.

VIRILIO. This is obviously an element that's completely beyond our understanding. Because we've seen plenty of things, but that . . . When we saw the first concentration camp survivors coming back . . . we couldn't believe our eyes.

BRAUSCH. Marguerite Duras has given a good account of the terrible wait in Paris at the Red Cross headquarters in the Hôtel Lutetia. Awaiting return to life or news of death. They were, at any rate, the living dead who came home. Duras shows this in the case of her own husband, Robert Antelme, telling how difficult it was for these people to return to life, taking food gramme by gramme at first, since their bodies weren't used to it and, otherwise, they too could have died . . .

VIRILIO. That was absolute horror. And then there was also an absolute escalation: there was Hiroshima. The war wouldn't go away.[15] And Hiroshima too—'that' wouldn't go away. We were happy. The war was over. I remember on the radio—and this is the same 'I remember' as Perec's because, as you very rightly said earlier, he too was a child of the war (he's my war brother and we each of us have a different, but parallel, 'I remember')—I remember having heard a nuclear explosion. I don't remember if it was Bikini Atoll . . . At any rate, 'it' came over as a crackling or, in other words, like 'static'—but we understood nothing about it, except for having an unconscious sense that it was space that was being rent asunder. Those who'd experienced the bombings understood; those who'd seen cities disappear understood; the sky's torn apart and bodies disintegrate. The atom bomb was an apocalyptic vision;

you couldn't be glad about it. Camus wrote immediately in the papers that it was a scandal, whereas others said, 'It had to be done, it's good.' We, I, who had lived through the war and the bombings, I repeat that we couldn't be glad on this occasion. It was too much. It was like the concentration camps. Auschwitz and Hiroshima are pendants to each other. They're organized death, and that's the supreme perversion of the human spirit.

BRAUSCH. What remains of them that's real is the shadow on a wall . . .

VIRILIO. Yes, a charred wall, with the shadow photographed by death. This is the 'illustration' of this technical milieu, as the same thing exists in the 'natural' state: take Pompeii and the natural explosion of Vesuvius in Antiquity. It's the same phenomenon again, but this time manufactured artificially, devised by the mind and hand of man: this space of war that has become a totalitarian space through the appearance and disappearance of things, creatures, cities, towns, villages, races, etc. People were destroyed in extermination camps, cities were destroyed—Guernica as much as Coventry, Rotterdam, Hiroshima, Hamburg or Dresden.

In 1945 we have in our hands the instrument with which we can destroy the world. Total war has become totalitarian war.

BRAUSCH. It also wrote the word 'end' under total war, which became the Cold War. That was another perversion, but one that maintained the peace for quite a long time by deploying a lethal threat. It's a perverse hope that's made it possible during the forty years of the Cold War not to despair totally of peace.

VIRILIO. Yes. The atom bomb became a weapon of deterrence, keeping the peace through absolute fear—fear of the end of the world.

And I'd remind you that my church at Nevers (we'll speak of this again later), which I designed with Claude Parent and which is shaped like a bunker, takes that form, because it refers to this collective fear of the end of the world. And since the church is dedicated to Bernadette Soubirous, Saint Bernadette of the Lourdes grotto, the theme I chose was that of the modern grotto—namely, the nuclear fallout shelter.

*Notes*

1   These interviews were first published in French and German in 1997, at which point Paul Virilio (born Paris, 1932) was director of the École spéciale d'architecture, and an author with many notable titles to his name and Marianne Brausch (born Luxembourg, 1955) was an urbanist, journalist and co-author (with Marc Emery) of *L'Architecture en questions* (Paris: Éditions du Moniteur, 1996).

2   'A Dieu' in the sense both of Adieu and 'I commend you to God.'

3   Gilles Deleuze, 'The Exhausted' in *Essays Critical and Clinical* (Daniel W. Smith and Michael A. Greco trans.) (London: Verso, 1998), pp. 152–3 (translation modified).

4   Louis-Ferdinand Céline was the pen name of French author Louis-Ferdinand Destouches (27 May 1894–1 July 1961).—Trans.

5   Paul Virilio, *L'Insécurité du territoire* (Paris: Stock, 1976).

6   Potemkin villages were purportedly fake settlements constructed to deceive Empress Catherine II of Russia on her visit to the Crimea in 1787. Historians now consider accounts of such villages questionable. —Trans.

7  Georges Perec, *Je suis né* (Paris: Editions de Seuil 1990).—Trans.

8  Georges Perec, *La vie, mode d'emploi* (Paris: Hachette, 1978); *Life: A User's Manual* (David Bellos trans.) (London: Vintage, 2003)

9  Duvignaud, who taught Perec, was the author of *Perec ou La cicatrice* (Arles: Actes Sud, 1993).—Trans.

10 Paul Virilio, *Guerre et cinéma* (Paris: Cahiers du cinéma/Editions de l'Etoille, 1984); *War and Cinema: The Logistics of Perception* (Patrick Camiller trans.) (London: Verso, 1989).—Trans.

11 This is the first line of 'L'adieu du cavalier' from Guillaume Apollinaire's *Calligrammes* (Paris: Mercure de France, 1918).—Trans.

12 Sébastien Le Prestre, Seigneur de Vauban, later Marquis de Vauban (1633–1707), commonly referred to as Vauban, was a Marshal of France and the foremost military engineer of his age, famed for his skill in designing fortifications. Between 1667 and 1707, he upgraded the fortifications of around 300 cities and directed the building of 37 new fortresses.—Trans.

13 Published for the first time for the exhibition *Bunker Archaeology: Paul Virilio* organized by the Centre for Industrial Creation and presented at

the Museum of Decorative Arts, Paris, from December 1975 to February 1976. The exhibition featured 180 photographs taken by Virilio between 1958 and 1965. It is now available as: *Bunker Archéologie* (Paris: Editions Galilée, 2008); *Bunker Archeology* (George Collins trans.) (New York: Princeton Architectural Press, 1994).—Trans.

14 The reference is to the chapel of Notre-Dame-du-Haut de Ronchamp near Belfort in Franche-Comté, Eastern France.—Trans.

15 The original French—'*ça passe pas*'—contains an allusion to the book by Henry Rousso and Éric Conan, *Vichy, un passé qui ne passe pas* (Paris: Messageries du livre, 1996).—Trans.

2
'IT'S THE INVISIBLE SPACE THAT
ENABLES US TO SEE THE VISIBLE'
*1950 or the Birth of the Thinker of the In-Between*

*The Nature that puts the mask of the visible on the
invisible is merely an appearance corrected by a
transparency.*
Victor Hugo

PAUL VIRILIO. After the war and the euphoria of
the Liberation came the discovery of the sea and
the infinite, of that space that was now unoccu-
pied once again, and the revelation of the bunker
monolith. I became contemplative. I wanted to
become a painter.

MARIANNE BRAUSCH. Was it to gain respite from the
shock of the space of speed (*l'espace vitesse*), the instability you experienced as a child during the war,

that you wanted to fix in your mind things that had, in a sense, got away from you? Were you trying to stop time or, at least, by painting, fix moments and then gain respite by looking at them?

VIRILIO. In a sense, to fix them in my mind so as to look at them. I became contemplative because, as a war child, I was a voyeur. I looked in a particular way. But, like Perec, who tried to find his way by working through in writing everything that he saw, I looked at everything with a sense of voyeurism, which prevented me from being an 'actor', from entering into the action of a 'normal' life. For me, then, the goal was to be a painter.

BRAUSCH. Why? You could have chosen another form of artistic expression. You could, like Perec, have written, since you'd already done so during the war . . .

VIRILIO. No, I wanted my 'self' to be active—even if that was a contemplative time. The means I chose were themselves active: the process went from my brain to my fingertips and back. In fact, I was an active thinker. My eyes were on my fingertips and I was trying to 'put things down' on a canvas. I'd remind you that, on account of the war and being knocked about from pillar to post by events, I was never able to establish a place for myself in the world except as someone looking on passively at events. My 'real', cultural education hadn't happened; my thinking wasn't structured. All the things of the mind were still to be discovered and I discovered painting—Picasso, Van Gogh and Cézanne—and also the theatre, through Sartre's play *The Flies*. And, as it happens, I worked with Nicolas Bataille on the sets for an adaptation of Rimbaud's *Season in Hell* at the Théâtre de Poche in Montparnasse.

BRAUSCH. Theatrical sets, wartime Potemkin cities—the quotation you chose as epigraph to this chapter was a good one: the 'invisible' puts on the 'mask of the visible' . . . and you were producing false *reality*, your real working world was barely even unreal . . .

VIRILIO. Yes, I was 'really' making the masks for this show. So I was discovering the world of art and, out of its multiple forms of expression, it was painting that won out, even if, since the end of the war (I was fourteen or fifteen), I'd been a voracious reader. I read a book a day . . .

But, to come back to painting, where, as you say, my real world was 'barely even unreal' (was that by chance?), it was in those years that the quarrel between figurative painters, for whom the form of the object was everything, and the abstract painters, who didn't represent the tangible world, was beginning. Now, for me, abstraction was real. I could make sense of things only when there was a figure, but I do mean 'a figure', not the figurative.

BRAUSCH. Was this a reflection of your war experience? Was it a 'product' of war, of destruction?

VIRILIO. Yes and no. It was an effect of the war on my vision of the destroyed, vanished world, as we said in the first of these interviews.

I had the impression of having lived through a carnival of appearances or, more precisely, a carnival of dislocation and, in a way, yes, I saw the world through that vision of destruction, since I'd stopped believing my eyes.

BRAUSCH. But there you're heading, nonetheless, towards the tangible.

VIRILIO. No, since my interest in the production of paintings went, first of all, towards still life. As I saw it, still life wasn't an exercise on objects and the way they're laid out within the space of the canvas but an exercise on the space between objects. The whole of my work would, in fact, be directed towards anti-form, to the gap between the objects, as I say in the introduction to *Negative Horizon*.[1] My work would lie at the meeting-point of the figurative and the abstract, since every form is both figurative, in the representation of the object, and abstract, in the transparency—that is to say, the gap—'between' things. I didn't do any special arranging of things. I painted what I had to hand and my interest was in what lay between the objects, between two poles. It was the effect between these poles, these anti-poles, that interested me.

BRAUSCH. You were painting, but your work was in fact an intellectual research programme. You were in search of a way of thinking.

VIRILIO. That's right. What I discovered through my work on still life was that, when I changed my position in space in relation to some object or other, then what I call the anti-form—or the interval, if you prefer—would widen and change shape. The objects remained what they were; they were mostly symmetrical and when you moved round them, that didn't change anything. But the shape between the objects, on the other hand, would change: it's a figure of displacement. To put it another way—and this is what interested me— the anti-form is the form of the travel or displacement of the observer. And this work on the reality of figurative objects would lead me into a jungle: the moving jungle of the gap that's constantly changing, that's always surprising, that's always developing, that's always made anew.

BRAUSCH. What interested you in fact wasn't painting, but—through your production—

things that moved . . . and yourself moving between them; what interested you was the seer who 'existed' between.

VIRILIO. Indeed it wasn't so much painting, but that particular space I was analyzing. And there's a logic in this, as what had interested me since the Second World War was the environment. And, in fact, that would bring me to architecture.

And in my movements around the city, the anti-form enabled me to find a nature. Nature isn't flowers, trees and rivers in the generic sense of the term, but this form of movement, this tropism of appearances which means that at a particular moment, at the place where I am and where I'm seeing only something ordinary, something extra-ordinary appears. At the time, in fact, I gave my paintings the title 'Between'. This would bring me to think through the space-between, the *entre-deux*. And this always puts me in mind of the Entre-Deux-Mers, that geographical space between the Bordelais and the Dordogne! . . .

BRAUSCH. Like the Bordeaux writer Pierre Veil-
let—and here we're back with writing and its
ambiguities too—who spelt the city of Bordeaux:
*Bords d'Eaux*, water's edges . . .

VIRILIO. Yes, it's this notion of interval, of *entre-
vaut*, in the sense of what is valid or of value
(*vaut*) between (*entre*) things . . . It was in fact a
philosophical labour.

BRAUSCH. Who were the philosophers who interested you at that time?

VIRILIO. Jean Wahl. Vladimir Jankélévitch with his
dear old 'certain somethings' and his 'scarcely any-
things', attentive as he was to the problem of *la
durée* and the moment—things that were very
important to me. Raymond Aron, whose critical,
relativistic philosophy of history—in the idea of the
'relative', there is doubt—couldn't but interest me,
since, to remind you once more, I'd stopped
believing my eyes. And, in my reading, Husserl.
And then Merleau-Ponty, whose research, I'd
remind you, was directed towards the unreflected
element in our perception of the world and the

description, not the explanation, of the real. He kept open the dialectic of history.

But I come back to my artistic work on the anti-form. This was very important. Without that thinking, I'd never have gone into architecture later. We'll see why in the next chapter.

BRAUSCH. Can we say that for you this was a time of silent writing?

VIRILIO. Exactly. It was different from a writing or a painting that brought something out. I'd call it a painting that set something down. It set down something fleeting, since it's in the nature of anti-form to disppear immediately. It's a setting down of something that's going to disappear and that appears [*qui va disparaître et qui apparaît*]: we're already in the 'ethics of disappearance' here; we're not in the world of static objects. And this is why I did still-life paintings: the objects in them had no other point than to be generators of space.

Of course, even if I exhibited a number of 'anti-forms', that didn't make me a living. I became a master glazier and had the good fortune to be able to work on Matisse's stained glass windows at Saint-Paul-de-Vence and Braque's windows at Varengeville. Clearly, working with masters like that was an extraordinary experience and learning process. I was lucky enough to have as a livelihood an activity in which I worked alongside great men, and then I met Le Corbusier at the time when he was working on the church at Ronchamp. For the glass at Ronchamp—it wasn't stained glass—he came to the Bony studio, where I was a master glazier. That meeting took place in 1958, at the point when I was starting my research into the bunkers of the Atlantic Wall. That was obviously very important for me, since there are obvious relations between the architecture of the bunkers and the architecture of Ronchamp, La Tourette, etc.

I was also taking an interest in physics at that time, a discipline we'll come back to later.

The work I was doing in the field of painting quite naturally led, as you've understood, to philosophy and to another view of space. And Vladmir Jankélévitch played a crucial role for me in this. Had it not been for Jankélévitch, I'd never have taught.

BRAUSCH. Why?

VIRILIO. Because listening to Jankélévitch was going to the opera! He was a master of language. He wasn't, perhaps, the greatest philosopher, but, alongside Lacan, he was the greatest orator I've ever heard. To hear him was to be taken out of yourself, the way you might be carried away by an operatic performance. And he was, in fact, a musician, a musicologist, and his way of speaking was musicological.

BRAUSCH. Let me interrupt you here, because I understand very well what you're saying. I encountered the same kind of learning process with my father, who was a musician and who initiated me into that art very early on. He taught me rhythm, breathing, punctuation, silences, tempi . . . and I transpose this quite naturally today into my way of writing. This may seem pretentious, but when I write I compose 'space-times'. It's almost physical.

VIRILIO. It was precisely that. The other philosopher who interested me at the time at a political level, and who is a war writer, was Raymond Aron. I attended his lectures, though I wasn't doing his course, when he was giving his *Eighteen Lessons on Industrial Society* and lecturing on 'Peace and War between the Nations' (he reversed Tolstoy's title). But the philosopher who most inspired me was Merleau-Ponty.

BRAUSCH. You've already mentioned him before, but if you'd like to explain again what significance he had for you . . .

VIRILIO. I found in him an echo of my German masters, who were the 'Gestaltists'. I discovered *Gestaltheorie* through Guillaume's book, *La psychologie de la forme*,[2] and then through the work of the Berlin School in general: Koffka, Lewin, Köhler and Wertheimer. Later on Kurt Lewin emigrated to the US and became one of the great figures of what became known as 'dynamic psychology'. Since I was a phenomenologist and a gestaltist, I was interested both in Merleau-

Ponty's phenomenology of perception and in the Gestalt theorists.

BRAUSCH. What do you understand by *Gestalt*? Everyone puts their head in their hands when it comes to translating the term! I'm often asked how to translate it. I reply 'right form' on account of the German root *Gestaltung*. The verb *gestalten* means to conceive, form, create . . .

VIRILIO. The definition of the *Gestalt* is the environment itself. With the military space and the space of my anti-forms, I find myself right inside it. To explain, there's no text without a context and the whole is more than the sum of its parts. I'll give you a very simple example of the *Gestalt*, if you like: when you take a lift with plain walls and you look at the wall, you can't help looking upwards if the lift is going down. It's as though there were a piece of elastic between the wall and the eyes of the person looking. Try it! That's *Gestalt*: when something passes in front of you—assuming you don't close your eyes—you can't help but be sucked in by the movement of that thing. Once again, it's another 'aesthetics of disappearance'.

It's logical then, as I've just said, that I should find the *Gestalt* in the military space, which is an environmental space. A bunker, for example, involves dead angles. That is to say, one place is concealed so as to uncover another. It's a 'field of perception'. War is a field of perception, so it's also a field of analysis for the phenomenology of perception.

To give you another example: what's camouflage? It's phenomenology of perception with the aim of deceiving the enemy gaze.

The field of philosophy that interested me was, quite naturally, phenomenological philosophy. And I very quickly lost interest in Sartre, in whom so many were interested at the time, but who is merely an epigone of Husserl. Even today, I'm not simply 'Merleau-Pontian' but 'Husserlian'. In my view, Husserl is the master and Heidegger remains the student. The fact that Heidegger was a Nazi doesn't interest me. I don't say, 'Since he was a Nazi, he's a bad philosopher.' But I do say,

'The Jew Husserl is a greater philosopher than Heidegger.'

BRAUSCH. At root, then, there's Husserl's relativism . . .

VIRILIO. Yes, because all my work was to be the work of a phenomenologist based on looking.

The phenomenology of perception is clearly about 'the visible and the invisible'. The last— very great—book by Merleau-Ponty, a book much loved by Deleuze and one I love myself, was *Le visible et l'invisible*.[3] All the work I've done since the war has been on this sleight of hand of reality: reality's elusive, it escapes, it's never stable. This is what interests me in phenomenology and *Gestalt* theory. I know that when I bring the two together like this, psychologists and philosophers will tell me they're not the same thing! In *Gestalt* theory, there's a more systematic dimension than in Husserl's or Merleau-Ponty's relativism. I agree on that point. Only, *Gestalt* taught me what I call 'the construction set'. And there I want to say that the Gestaltists were structuralists before structuralism—long before. And this is why I never became a structuralist in the years of the great structuralists—in the '60s with Lévi-Strauss, etc. I'd learned, thanks to the Gestaltists that you had both to recognize structure . . . and then beware of it!

BRAUSCH. As of any exact science . . .

VIRILIO. Yes, of any allegedly exact philosophy. Some were Marxists, I was a Gestaltist!

BRAUSCH. Clearly, you weren't tempted at all by Wittgenstein.

VIRILIO. Not at all. But I did, on the other hand, become passionate about physics, which I even conflated with philosophy. At that time I read everything—Heisenberg, Dirac, de Broglie, Einstein, Schrödinger. I was excited because all of that fitted together. They too were working on relativity.

BRAUSCH. So mathematics, at least when defined as an exact science, left you cold.

VIRILIO. Totally. Geometry interested me, of course. But arithmetic . . . Sadly, set theory wasn't yet being taught.

BRAUSCH. I'll break in here to say that I did have that opportunity. I must have had at least as great an interest as you in mathematics—that is to say, no interest at all—but I was excited by set theory—by the ellipses, by what went on between them when they met, overlapped, intersected . . . Of course I failed my baccalaureate. But to get into the architecture school where I studied—Saint-Luc in Brussels (this was in 1974)—there was an entrance exam that you could take if you didn't have your *bac'* and I sat it. The maths teacher understood that, since I was excited by set theory, I understood the 'in-between', as you put it, and hence space. They gave me a place at the architecture school and the question of re-sitting my baccalaureate never arose again. He even came to see me in the studio to see how I put my organigrammes together, how I related functions to one another, and then how I turned this into space, into architecture.

VIRILIO. I wasn't so lucky! But, to come back to physics, physics is also a form of writing. Louis de

Broglie's writing attracted me immediately. De Broglie was what Foucault has been to some extent for the rising generation—that is to say, a very fine stylist. At the time I'd read *Matière et lumière* (Matter and Light) and *Continu et discontinu en physique moderne* (Continuous and Discontinuous in Modern Physics). Once again, this ran along the lines of the thinking I was trying to develop and it introduced me to quantum space, probabilistic space. And then another important person for me was the British physicist Paul Dirac, who first had the idea of antimatter. I was, of course, already converted by the war, converted to the relativity of things, since 'I no longer believed my eyes' and the 'view on . . .' was crucial to me—we've been speaking of this throughout this interview. At that point, the theory of antimatter confirmed my view of the world as twofold: a world made up of objects and a world of trajects; a world of light and shade; of form and anti-form; of matter and antimatter. All this confirmed the thinking I was engaged on at the time. But in the 1950s this seemed very fanciful. Only physicists believed in such things as matter and antimatter. It was still pretty hard at the time to believe in space-time, in the space-time continuum!

BRAUSCH. Certainly. And let's just take the example of the painting you were working on. What were the figurative and abstract painters to think of relativism?

VIRILIO. It was another world, a world that couldn't coexist with that one. In other words, it was an explosive world. A German scientist recently managed to preserve some particles of anti-matter for a few fractions of a second and he was immediately devastated by the questions he was asked by journalists. Naturally, they asked him, 'Can you make a bomb with it?' The antimatter bomb would indeed be a hundred times more powerful than the atom bomb . . . It's a world that cannot, then, coexist with our own.

Naturally, I wasn't looking at antimatter from that point of view. Nevertheless, it interested me in terms of the splitting of reality.

BRAUSCH. That is to say, there are, in your view, two worlds that coexist—the 'real' world and the 'abstract' world, but in the real sense too. The abstract world has its reality.

VIRILIO. Exactly, it's what's now called the quantum world. Quantum physics has shown us that there was a kind of Russian doll, within which systems were embedded that differed in nature, but obviously coexisted. Except in the case of antimatter.

BRAUSCH. You put me in mind of Hannah Arendt here, who, in her book *Men in Dark Times*, wrote about Walter Benjamin—this is Jewish mysticism, obviously—that he saw the whole world in two grains of wheat. Like a written formula that would contain within it all possible writing. And I've just discovered a magnificent quotation from Duras' last book *La mer écrite*: 'What else could one show other than what one sees? That which is simply true and eludes human beings.' That's fantastic, isn't it? I was 'staggered' by it, as they say. My whole thinking is subsumed in this; in a single phrase or in the philosopher Walter Benjamin's grain of rice.[4] The fragment is all and everything is in the fragment: it's an 'elusive' reality (like a fish that slips through your hands)!

VIRILIO. The macrocosm in the microcosm and vice versa . . .

And naturally, this interest in painting, an exploratory, not an expository painting . . .

BRAUSCH. . . . a research into the tension between things . . .

VIRILIO. . . . has to do, above all, with the light space—not the space of half-light, of chiaroscuro, but space in the sense of Paolo Ucello or Piero della Francesca who, in working on perspective, worked on light and light rays. There's a work of another kind here that will be seen again in architecture, in the tension of modern architecture.

BRAUSCH. Yes, listening to you speak, I'm not hearing or seeing those 'white volumes in the light' of Le Corbusier that are so dear to our archaeo-Corbusians!

VIRILIO. You're right. My interest in relativism, in anti-form (which has nothing to do with Le Corbusier's realist conception with regard to the opaqueness of matter!), separated me very quickly from the painters. Because the Paris School, as it was called at the time (I'm not denigrating it, there are some very great painters among them), was of no interest to me: it was concerned only with surface effects. In other words, I didn't find structure or geometry there, in the physical sense of the term. In that sense, I'm a Florentine: those who interest me are Francesca and Ucello. My work was aimed, so to speak, in that direction: it ran counter to all that was being done and thought at the time.

By contrast, architecture was beginning to go in that direction.

BRAUSCH. You were interested by the plastic arts . . .

VIRILIO. By the sculptors—Moore, Giacometti, etc.

BRAUSCH. And Le Corbusier, plastic artist and sculptor.

VIRILIO. I'd remind you that all this came about through a conscientious objection. I was a relativist: I had a 'conscientious objection'. As I saw it, reality was like a theatre set. And that's why Victor Hugo's phrase suits me perfectly: 'Nature which puts the mask of the visible—the scenery —on the invisible is simply an appearance corrected by a transparency.' I very quickly realized that there were two interlocking architectures: the architecture of fullness (walls, built volumes) and the architecture of emptiness.

BRAUSCH. This was what brought us together, how we came to know each other and recognize each other's work, when we were both editing series for the Éditions du Demi-Cercle! For a long time I'd known Colin Rowe's essay on transparency, 'Transparency Real and Phenomenal'. In France, of course, no one was aware of it; the French are such realists! So I was able to translate that essay, which was a minor bombshell, some forty years after it was written, and publish it in your series . . .

VIRILIO. Yes, things sometimes take their time! But, to come back to the subject, this architecture of fullness and architecture of emptiness is true in two dimensions. And also true in three, with architectural volumetrics.

BRAUSCH. And also in terms of depth or, in other words, of superimposed transparencies. And it's not by chance that you knew and worked with Braque, who reworked the three-dimensional object on the two-dimensional canvas, suggesting the multiplicity of viewpoints.

VIRILIO. That's right. Another important aspect at the time was that, in the 1960s, I was doing Zen-like exercises. In the Metro I worked at forgetting what was around me. I tried to feel the space and not the people.

BRAUSCH. Yes . . . reading your preface to *Negative Horizon*, I thought of the Japanese tradition of unrolling a painting and meditating for a while on its content and meaning, then putting it away and beginning over again. The Zen 'exercise' is, of course, much more than that—it's a philosophy of life that gives the moment a sense of eternity. We might compare this order of thinking with our Western conception of the void, the fragment and the fractal . . .

VIRILIO. Painting exists in the moment and not just in the space of the picture: it exists in space-time. This is precisely what I mean by *The Aesthetics of Disappearance*, one of my first books of the 1980s (don't forget that I began publishing late).[5] From that point on, I was less interested in the aesthetics of appearance. Disappearance or non-appearance was much more important for me than exhibition . . .

BRAUSCH. Ex-posure, over-exposure . . .

VIRILIO. Yes, and disappearance, under-exposure. This confirms what I often say: I believe more in the evidence of the implicit than the evidence of the explicit. These are things that would leave their mark in my later work, in the work on architecture, on technological space, etc. That's what I can say about that period and its consequences.

There are lots more things to say. We could go much further. On post-war cinema, for example. In my view, it's summed up in a single film: *Hiroshima mon amour*.

BRAUSCH. Why?

VIRILIO. It's a film that blows all the others away. It marks the break with the past. Before that, I went to the cinema the way you go to the town square: I went out with friends for three hours to see some westerns! Not for John Wayne's sake, but to see a landscape that was different from what we had in the street. It was 'being in a public square in a darkened room'. But it wasn't cinema, in the sense of an 'art of seeing'. We went to see the big empty spaces. Post-war life was still very frugal— I was poor, I lived in Aubervilliers. And then came *Hiroshima mon amour*: the break with the past.

BRAUSCH. You were escaping from a life where nothing happened—this time in the real sense of the term!

VIRILIO. Marguerite Duras and Alain Resnais's *Hiroshima mon amour* represented a very distinct break. And then came Resnais's *Night and Fog* (*Nuit et brouillard*). But *Night and Fog*, which was so hard, took us back to what we'd already seen and left less of a mark. Whereas *Hiroshima mon amour* was something else: the delta-shaped estuary of the Ota river. And what was the view that it gave us? It was an aerial view from flying over the Hiroshima delta. There's Duras' phrase that I've never forgotten, '*Dans l'embouchure en delta du fleuve Ota*', over aerial shots of the Ota river.

BRAUSCH. You realized, in fact, that your experience of the war could be transposed into the imaginary register. The real is unreal and the unreal is the equal of the real . . .

VIRILIO. This was a vision that would mark my book *War and Cinema*. For once one had an aerial vision of what one had experienced on the ground. Even if Nantes wasn't Hiroshima, we'd lived through that! That went in the direction of travel of the thinking on the 'real/unreal' that I was developing. It was a sublimation. It was the absolute of the real/abstract and of a free form of figuration through a love story. This Japanese man and French woman finding each other expressed the ambiguity of what we'd lived through during the war: it was the metaphor of mythical figures; it wasn't a private vision but a historical one that lent a whole period its identity.

BRAUSCH. It was filmed, visualized philosophy.

VIRILIO. Yes, that's crucial. And then there was that extreme slowness that took on such proportions—which unfurled space like a carpet or a Japanese painting. For me it was something self-evident that enabled me to be reconciled with myself—with my equivalent view of the world.

BRAUSCH. After that, you'd see cinema differently, since there'd also be Italian Neo-realism (the term is so right).

VIRILIO. Yes, those films helped me once again to see reality—reality being merely a figuration.

BRAUSCH. Up to that point, you were working on (with) tangible things—painting, sculpture, architecture—and suddenly there was the image, which would take up the whole of space in the contemporary world, leading eventually to the 'absent', virtual image which makes up today's world (and I use that verb advisedly), on which subject you were to become one of the essential thinkers. And all this thanks to the shock of *Hiroshima mon amour* and the shock of the bunkers, which also confirmed what you were as a flesh-and-blood individual, even if you no longer wished to 'see'. Whether tangible (the action also takes place at Nevers where—by chance?—you built a church) or immaterial, it was the 'thought-through' meaning that counted for you, the in-between . . . which you 'saw'! That's what it means to be relativistic, isn't it?

VIRILIO. Yes, and this gives you a great openness towards the world. A great freedom of life and thought, which are, indeed, one and the same, as you well know, since that is why we 'met' and are able to hold this dialogue!

*Notes*

1  Paul Virilio, *L'horizon négatif. Essai de dromosco-pie* (Paris: Galilée, 1984); *Negative Horizon: An Essay in Dromoscopy* (Michael Degener trans.) (London: Continuum, 2006)

2  Paul Guillaume, *La psychologie de la forme* (Paris: Flammarion, 1937).

3  Maurice Merleau-Ponty, *Le Visible et l'invisible, suivi de notes de travail* (Paris: Gallimard, 1964); *The Visible and the Invisible, Followed by Working Notes* (Alphonso Lingis trans.) (Evanston: Northwestern University Press, 1968).

4  The reference earlier was to wheat rather than rice, but I have resisted the temptation to 'clean up' such small discrepancies in the text.—Trans.

5  Paul Virilio, *Ésthétique de la disparition* (Paris: Galilée, 1980); *The Aesthetics of Disappearance* (New York: Semiotext(e), 1991).

3

ON THE OBLIQUE AS A PRINCIPLE OF LIFE:
FROM BUNKER TO 'FREE PLAN'
*1960*: *War and Peace*

*Architecture is the art of concealment.*
Paul Virilio

PAUL VIRILIO. It's the art of keeping something in
one's possession . . .

We're in the mid-60s here, 1965–66, and I
moved from the art of painting to that of architecture. In my sketchbooks I wasn't drawing still
lifes any more, but living spaces and, naturally,
bunkers, which had left a permanent impression
on me, studying bunker architecture as I had since
1958. It was work that wasn't just concerned with
the archaeological aspect of the Second World

War, but the military space of 'Fortress Europe' with its *Reichsautobahnen* (the Third Reich's motorways), the rocket-launching sites, the *Luftschützräume* (air-raid shelters) and the first radar installations—in a word, the *territory*.

MARIANNE BRAUSCH. So you were working on the topology of horizontal space and on three-dimensional space—you were working 'in' three dimensions.

VIRILIO. Yes, the architectural and the urban dimensions. In fact, in 1963 I created the group *Architecture Principe* with the architect Claude Parent (he was already a member of other groups like *Espace*, founded by André Bloc), the sculptor Maurice Lipsi and the painter Michel Carrade. It was a time when there was a lot of talk of multi-disciplinary working groups and efforts to bring together painters, sculptors and so on. It was the time of the 'cultural community' that would lead to the Cultural Revolution of May '68 and, in China, for those who were Maoists at the time, to the 'Long March' of the revolutionary students.

BRAUSCH. What particularly attracted you?

VIRILIO. The knowledge of geostrategy and geopolitics, which I'd experienced—or rather been subjected to—as a child in Nantes. For me, war architecture illustrated the whole power of technology and fortifications rendered perceptible the—now cosmic—dimensions of destructive power.

BRAUSCH. We have to say that you were a *Gestalt-theorie* enthusiast . . .

VIRILIO. Very much so. I was, as a result, familiar with the 'psychology of form' and the 'phenomenology of perception'. That approach to conflict-space enabled me better to understand the extreme importance of logistics and, hence, the circulatory flows of the *Blitzkrieg* era. And also of balistics and projectiles in the configuration of the military architecture of the times, which I covered in my book *Speed and Politics*.[1] So I was already beginning to see the possibility of a topological (I stress the term) or, at least, a non-orthogonal architectonics.

BRAUSCH. Were you just doing theoretical research or did this find a concrete embodiment?

VIRILIO. That was the time when I got the commission for a parish centre in Nevers from his Grace Bishop Vial, who would eventually become bishop of Nantes and be buried in the crypt of Nantes cathedral. With the Nantes of my childhood and the Nevers of *Hiroshima mon amour*, we're in a curious charmed circle. From Nevers, by way of Hiroshima, we get back to Nantes . . . anecdotally speaking, and symbolically too, I've come full circle and that's a hard fact to face! Yet it's a curious mark of destiny because the parish centre is dedicated to Saint Bernadette. By a strange coincidence, the name of Bernadette (Soubirous) brings us to the grotto at Lourdes and the grotto brings us, of course, to the crypt—that is to say, to a terrifying place. The cave or grotto is the place of mere appearances, but also the place of terror and the place where the first human beings created their art.

BRAUSCH. Terrifying in one sense perhaps, but also a happy coincidence. You're always telling me that 'the Angel has settled on my shoulder' . . . On yours too. I'm thinking of the philosopher Walter Benjamin, a man of such tragic destiny, but with so rich a life, a life so full of sudden flashes of genius. He lived his life 'under the sign of' (under the protection of or, better, under exposure to) Klee's painting of the angel of the apocalypse.[2] He knew that his thinking was dynamite, especially for his friend and (nonetheless) enemy, Adorno, and the Frankfurt School. They were orthodox Marxists and he was a free thinker like you. His fate was a cruel one— he lived it through to the end. Yours announced itself, despite your wartime beginnings, a little more auspiciously!

VIRILIO. Yes. Because it was clear to me that this grotto of Lourdes would be the metaphor I'd introduce: the bunker. The atomic bunker. I'd remind you that in the 1960s we were fully in the age of deterrence. It was all about the balance of terror. So, the atomic bunker was the crypt of the obsession with—and the fear of—extermination.

BRAUSCH. Collective fear again, as in the Second World War. Though tempered by an 'anecdotal' fact that I find ultimately funny, absurd and optimistic. We know that, at that time, some among the ultra-rich had personal bunkers built for themselves, the way Noah built his Ark before the flood! Human nature will simply never lose hope: life will always be stronger than death. What a pity man has in him the 'sign' of evil, of domination and that there should always—even in time of peace—be a war going on . . .

VIRILIO. Yes. It was precisely this terror I wanted to leave its stamp on the church. I took my inspiration here from the consecration ceremony for churches, which begins with the word *terribilis*: 'How dreadful is this place'.[3] Every time a Christian church is consecrated, preparations are made for a church service entitled *'Terribilis'*. That's extraordinary.

It so happens also that I was in Germany at that time, at Düsseldorf, Hamburg and elsewhere, and I saw bunkers, *Luftschutzräume*, transformed into churches.

BRAUSCH. When I was studying architecture in the 1970s—and this is a sign of the times—I often went to Amsterdam, where churches and chapels were being turned into discothèques and rock-music venues. The Dutch always were 'ahead of things'—in this case, of our consumer civilization and its spiritual anti-values!

VIRILIO. But at the time I'm speaking of, it was the other way round: since the churches had been wrecked, the spaces made by the war were turned to Christian ends. In Düsseldorf, in particular, a bunker-church had been consecrated as the Church of the Holy Sacrament.

BRAUSCH. For me, and for you too—though you've just cited an example opposite in nature to mine—these were extraordinary signs!

VIRILIO. I was re-reading the prophet Isaiah yesterday. The Old Testament has a resonance with me as something I've lived through. And that you've lived through too.

BRAUSCH. I'd say rather that we've been given a gift for looking, and I don't know either why or how—except from our heightened sense of obser-vation and deduction, like Walter Benjamin, who is, as you know, one of the thinkers I most admire.

VIRILIO. Everything is in looking and in the word, but through the body's senses in their entirety. Now, the Bible is the Word. You have to read the prophets and read Christ—'live' them through your senses and your intelligence.

BRAUSCH. That is so true. I was reading a piece yesterday by Daniel Libeskind, the Polish Jewish architect, who's a friend of ours. He notes that, in Schönberg's opera *Moses and Aaron*, Aaron says: 'O words that fail me! O words that fail me!' and Schönberg could find no musical equivalent for this. Music destroyed this litany of the 'void', of the 'nothing' that is the 'all'.

VIRILIO. Good point! At the time, there was, of course, a great deal of talk of the *balance* of terror, but what would interest Claude Parent and myself was *imbalance*, disequilibrium, life on inclined planes. We were taken with the idea that the age of the orthogonal was past and that one could live on oblique surfaces, that we could effectively envisage going beyond the postural reference of the classical age and orthogonality: the standing man. Beyond the 'dogma of the right angle', as Le Corbusier would say.

BRAUSCH. You're well aware that Le Corbusier, who is sadly the hero and model of French architecture—and will remain so for a long time—is 'my' personal enemy. He's the dogmatic individual I fear most, the worst anti-freedom architect I know. As the young of today would say, I feel a lot of 'aggro' towards him! Yet I'm not against Le Corbusier the sculptor; that's something else altogether. But, architecturally, he's the opposite of Christian Dior, who liberated women from their corsets.

VIRILIO. Yes, that's one way of putting it. And all the work of the *Architecture Principe* group was to be opposed to orthogonality and Euclidian architecture. The oblique function, which we'll talk about in a moment, is linked to that. This is important because the oblique function was perceived by many people as a formalism. It isn't a formalism! It's a culture of the body that plays on disequilibrium, that regards man not as static but in motion and takes the dancer as the model of the human being.

BRAUSCH. I'll interrupt you here because it seems to me I've an important anecdote to relate. When Adolf Loos set off for the US—this is still in the nineteenth century—he didn't have the money to pay for his passage. So, to pay his crossing, he became a dancing companion on a transatlantic liner! More seriously, though, Loos—another genius—is one of your precursors with his *Raum-Plan* (space-plan) houses, designed to match the various rhythms and movements of human beings over the course of the day. He's also one of your precursors in the realm of ideas. You're aware, no doubt, of the meaning of the bare facade of the Michaelerplatz building in Vienna? It was the outer 'skin' between the private man, who was free to do as he liked in his own home, and the public man with social responsibilities. Yet, he thought—and this must have been very provocative for the times—that human beings weren't intellectually mature enough for this. So he left the completion of the Michaelerplatz facade to a future generation of responsible men. That was when Freud was having his work cut out with Vienna's bourgeois women, whom Klimt represented so marvellously at the decorative level but so hieratically as to suggest that they must have been rather 'uptight'!

VIRILIO. Precisely, since those bourgeois women are closely akin to Le Corbusier's 'standing man' in *The Modulor*.[4]

The 'oblique function', as we shall call it, would clearly have need of a manifesto. This would be published in 1966 under the title *Architecture Principe*.[5] Thirty years later, the complete text of all nine parts of this manifesto—my *Bunker Archeology* was the seventh of them—was republished. In parallel with that publication came building projects—admittedly, very few in number—that were nonetheless to lend emphasis to the theoretical work of our research group. With

Parent I founded the Architecture Principe agency, which would have four projects. Only two of these were built: the church at Nevers and the Aerospace Research Centre for the Thomson-Houston group at Vélizy. The two others came to nothing: the Charleville project and the project for the Mariotti house at Saint-Germain-en-Laye, where we'd gone so far as to study the 'angling' of the inclined planes.

BRAUSCH. It was perhaps a partial failure and certainly didn't bring you great fame, but I know of a certain Jean Nouvel who worked for that agency and who has never forgotten that it was Parent who 'launched' his career, at a point when he knew nothing of architectural practice. He learned everything on the job and this is how he proceeds with the young people who work in his agency today. And a certain Paul Virilio is still one of his intellectual friends . . . Happily, Nouvel put a bomb under the archaeo-Corbusians' drawing boards! That may have been down to you! So thank you Claude Parent, thank you Paul Virilio!

VIRILIO. Yes, in the same way as Nouvel has his young architects gain experience on the building site itself, Parent and I attempted a life-size experiment on the oblique function. Our project, which was called *Pendular Destabilizer no. 1*, allowed Parent and myself to live for several weeks on oblique surfaces in a space we'd built at Nanterre. We wanted to test out—under medical supervision—the question of the equilibration of sloping surfaces and the extent to which it was possible to live on them, in order to determine our choice of angles for living spaces. But the May '68 events prevented us from seeing this psycho-physiological experiment through.

BRAUSCH. Can you say a bit more about this?

VIRILIO. At the origins of the theory of the 'oblique function' there's the idea of disequilibrium and motor instability. The idea that terrestrial gravity is an engine to be used. Hence the—very Galilean—proposal to make use of the inclined plane and to use 'horizontality' solely as a 're-balancing point' between two slopes. It seemed logical to us that, after the horizontal order of the rural habitat and the vertical order of the industrial habitat, the third order should be the oblique one of the post-industrial era. With the vertical walls 'disappearing' this way, the space would have been entirely accessible, thus increasing the usable surface-area: this was the principle of habitable circulation. You know that what's interested me since the 1940s and '50s has been movement, whether it's the movement of ballistics, mechanical engines or human beings. Another very important thing, which also came out of my experience of the topsy-turviness of aerial and terrestrial space during the war, was the end of the front/back opposition, since the only opposition that remains with oblique floors is that between top and bottom, between upper and lower surfaces. I've called this 'metastability', since, with the mobility in space of the body and the on-the-spot mobility of the individual's organs, then, thanks to the energy of disequilibrium, the inhabitant's body becomes locomotory. Our concept of oblique architecture was, then, a sort of generator of activities that used bodily techniques to promote habitability. Merleau-Ponty said, 'It isn't the eye that sees, but the body as open totality.' Hence our resolve within the *Architecture Principe* group to increase—by virtue of the topology of oriented surfaces—the number of genuinely liveable surfaces.

BRAUSCH. Let's come back to the two projects that were actually built and their significance.

VIRILIO. They represent the two ends of a metaphorical chain—of peace and war. The 'temple', in the fundamental sense, was clearly the church at Nevers, which takes the form of a heart with its two ventricles. This stands for life. And then there's the Thomson-Houston factory commission. That was a major building project, but the architects—and this is how things were done at the time—weren't aware of what the factory would be used for, except insofar as specific functions and the square-metreage were concerned. We were told it was an electronics research factory . . .

BRAUSCH. And you're going to tell me, it was a factory for . . .

VIRILIO. . . . . manufacturing homing warheads! In other words, it was a factory where they were working on missiles!

BRAUSCH. Chance really doesn't exist, does it? No one escapes his destiny and yours is, in part, a 'war' destiny, if I may put it that way!

VIRILIO. In the Gospels there's a verse that runs as follows—this is Christ addressing Peter—'upon this rock I will build my church; and the gates of hell shall not prevail against it'. Curiously, I have the impression of having built both these things: the church and the gates of hell.

BRAUSCH. I want to 'console' you by telling a parable that comes from a friend of mine who lives in Jerusalem. He took me up to the Mount of Olives, which gives you an almost complete view of the city walls. Opposite the Mount of Olives there's a famous cemetery where Jews and Christians were—and still are—buried. Why? The city of Jerusalem has seven gates; now, the parable says that on the Day of Judgement the prophet Elijah will enter Heavenly Jerusalem by the Seventh Gate. Of course—and here we're back with wars and the worst of them, wars of religion—the Muslims have walled up the gate. But what I want to tell you is this. On the Last Day, the prophet Elijah will enter Heavenly Jerusalem by the Seventh Gate. A bridge of paper and a bridge of iron will stretch across the Valley of Kidron. The just will follow Elijah over the bridge of paper and will be received by God, while the others will take the bridge of iron, which will collapse into the valley of Hell . . . Isn't that relativism? So, to come back to you, let's say you've accepted relativism, since you've built for both peace and war! It's almost Nietzschean: 'Good and Evil'.

VIRILIO. Since we're talking about bridges, I'd like to say this. It was our view that movement—the *traject*—was at last gaining the upper hand over the architectural *object*. The bridging structure made it possible to free up the landscape to the maximum thanks to the non-Euclidian geometry of large inclined arches. So, the sixth issue of the journal presented our 'Topo-tonics', great bridging structures stretching out 100 or 200 metres above a protected territory. This is how we came to the idea—which we'll talk about—of the 'living ground'.

BRAUSCH. This is all very interesting. Like Archigram's research work, which issued in just the one actual built project, the Centre Georges Pompidou (Beaubourg Centre). Do you have any regrets?

VIRILIO. I built nothing else and, in a way, it's a very good thing that I didn't. War overtook me again . . . Then came May '68, as I've said. The group was dissolved and Parent and I went our separate ways. Perhaps we were too futuristic? To close this interview, I'd like to come back to the theory we held and ensure that it's properly understood. One of the important elements of the oblique function was habitable circulation as opposed to habitable 'quartering' (*stationnement*).

As we saw it, orthogonality favoured non-movement. Stability, the horizontal plane and the vertical planes, linked to the statics of gravity, led to habitable quartering—not to say, 'human parking lots' . . .

BRAUSCH. Parking places, cattle trucks, deportation . . .

VIRILIO. Yes, it was also perhaps an unconscious reaction to the deportation to concentration camps—at any rate, to totalitarianism and the totalitarian world. We tried to bring gravity into play, to put bodies on—very slight—slopes, so as to lend them gravity's dynamic. It was, in a way, a move from Euclidian, orthogonal architecture, in which the planes are fixed, to non-Euclidian, topological architecture, in which the surfaces are oriented and concealed. We wanted to get beyond the tower, the vertical structure . . .

BRAUSCH. . . . the watchtower? . . .

VIRILIO. . . . which is the height of orthogonality and surveillance . . .

BRAUSCH. . . . of pride . . .

VIRILIO. . . . the Tower of Babel. We wanted, then, to move towards the bridge. You spoke of this metaphorically a moment ago—to the bridge and to bridging structures of all kinds. In the oblique function, everything has to be climbed; the walls, the furniture built into the floor . . .

BRAUSCH. This is the active wall, the action wall.

VIRILIO. It's what we called 'living ground'. At the same time, in 1966, we were invited to Berlin by Hans Scharoun and we visited the Philharmonie, which is all about fluidity of space. Scharoun was perhaps my only teacher where architecture was concerned. No, there were two: the bunkers and Hans Scharoun. Of course the two are poles apart: they are war and peace.

*Notes*

1 Paul Virilio, *Vitesse et politique* (Paris: Edition Galilée, 1977); *Speed and Politics* (Mark Polizotti trans.) (New York: Semiotext(e), 1977).—Trans.

2 A reference to Paul Klee's painting 'Angelus Novus', which Benjamin purchased in 1921.—Trans.

3 A reference to the introit 'Terribilis est locus iste', which is taken from Genesis 28: 17. This is the King James Bible translation.—Trans.

4 Le Corbusier, *The Modulor* (London: Faber & Faber, 1954).

5 Paul Virilio and Claude Parent, *Architecture Principe 1966 and 1996* (George Collins trans.) (Besançon/ Los Angeles: Les Éditions de l'Imprimeur/Form Zero Editions, 1996).

4

FROM GLOBALIZATION
TO THE PLANET'S LAST GALLOP
*1980 or the Desire to be Hungry in spite of Everything*

*The origin is the end.*
Karl Kraus

PAUL VIRILIO. I've chosen the epigraph to this last chapter in your honour, since you're just back from a trip to *Mitteleuropa*—to Prague in particular—and the political and cultural situation in the former Soviet Bloc is changing. But changing how? We don't know, as indeed we don't know how things are changing between the West and the former Yugoslavia, or in Africa, or between Israel and the Palestinians—in short, how they're changing in the world we live in. But we have to live all the same, and to do so this time with our eyes open to the real, after having learned not to believe our eyes.

MARIANNE BRAUSCH. The origin is the end (*la fin*). Is the origin also hunger (*la faim*)?[1]

VIRILIO. I shan't respond to that question right now, except to say 'yes' where creation is concerned. It constitutes, so to speak, the last word to this last chapter and I'll reply to it at the end of today's dialogue. But I'd say, right now, that these word games have to become meaning games. And it's clear that the end is when we've absorbed everything. But the origin is when we want to absorb everything . . . 'the origin is the end' because we're in a state of permanent war. However, we ought not to dis-hope, to despair. This will be one of the key points of this chapter, linked to survival. I'm inclined to say right away that desire and its satisfaction create a space between them: that space is called life.

BRAUSCH. What you've just said is, as I see it, a response in the liturgical sense. It resonates like an echo that nourished our previous dialogues and will 'nourish' the whole of the present interview. And I stress that it does so in a positive way, since you're too often described as a 'bird of ill omen' or a 'prophet of the Apocalypse'—even today (see the 'Rebonds' column of the Paris newspaper *Libération* of 23 May 1996). Knowing you—and leaving aside the question of your words being misinterpreted—you must be rather flattered by this: you're a 'disturber of the public peace', as was Kraus, the friend of Loos and Schönberg in early twentieth-century Vienna! Moreover, you're always hungry—and so am I— whatever the outcome awaiting us! May those who wish to be hungry after reading us still remain so! But, for that, one needs a particular awareness of the way the world is going. Now, as we know, most people prefer to shut their eyes and stop up their ears where the real is concerned.

VIRILIO. Before we go on, I'd like to say that this last chapter is a genuine dialogue between you and me, and that you're a member of a different generation, even if we both have a kind of twinned 'awareness' that bears no relation to the generation gap. But it does so happen that you're from another generation by the chance fact of our respective birth dates. Our respective experiences are, therefore, different and that affects our perception and interpretation of the world. And this will feed into the present interview.

So far as the previous three interviews are concerned, I'd like to say that they pained me somewhat, as I don't like to delve into the past. I'm not a man of the past. Nor am I a futurologist, a 'sorceror', as some people assert. I'm a man of the present and I would say almost, in response to those people, that I'm not a sorceror but a seeker after sources. As regards the past, all that was difficult for me. But things did happen; we have to remember them and go back over them. It had to be done.

In this last chapter, however, your questions will be entirely your own, as a young woman of the late twentieth century. And my answers will refer only to the present, fuelled, of course, by our personal thinking and sensibilities regarding the work that concerns us here. We shan't be referring to what *was* in the past but to what *is* in this moment of dialogue.

BRAUSCH. So we're going to speak, naturally, of architecture, of territory—both in the extended sense and in the sense of the street—of the media in general, of cinema and television, of society in general and of particular events—for example, the two-speed or multi-speed society (whatever the views of the false optimists—sadly, often our political leaders—who see the future as a linear progression, though we know their electoralist reasons for that)—of deconstrucivism in philosophy and architectural deconstructivism. In a word, and I say this advisedly, we're going to speak of the world as it is. And here I'm not asking for a response or echo from you, but for an answer. One of today's essential parameters is memory, while lies and negationism are its pendant. I don't dare speak of morality in this connection, because of the religious connotation. I'll speak, therefore, of 'ethics'.

It so happens that I met Elie Wiesel in Prague. We spoke about the 90,000 Czech Jews out of the 100,000 who lived in the 'Jerusalem of the West', who were deported and died—a necessarily painful memory—and we spoke about the present. Naturally, we talked also of the peace that's needed in the Middle East and of the dialogue he had with Jorge Semprun on the concentration camps, in which Semprun was imprisoned for his political opinions, a dialogue broadcast on the Franco-German Arte TV channel and now available in book form as *Se taire est impossible*.[2]

I'd like to say, from the outset, that memory—a certain, consciously worked-over memory is good and progressive, because it leads both inwards and onwards; just as melancholy, a certain form of melancholy—Dürer's famous 'black ink'—leads thinkers to think and writers to write—in short, leads creative artists to create.

This is obviously not without its pain and life is self-evidently not painless. We have to be able to give birth—being conscious of this, so as to be positive—in order to 'be in the world' in the original Greek philosophical sense of maieutics . . . We have to remember in order to move forwards and find an opening on to the present, even if we're moving towards an inevitable end!

VIRILIO. Let's begin, then, with this philosophical question in our society—our society that absorbs more than it gives and reduces the opening you speak of to the size of a needle's eye! What room does it leave, then, for the individual, the private 'human being' and the public 'citizen'? The answer to that question can be summed up in a few words: self-regulated freedom, civics, ethics. But your question is very complex and we have to whet our appetite for it, to take an *apéritif*, so to speak. As I usually do, then, I'll start from distant things in order to get to matters near at hand.

I do, in fact, believe that the question of memory is back on the agenda today, because it compels us to question things—in the sense we've just spoken of: in other words, ethically—but also, and most importantly, because it's now being exploited mechanically. I discussed this at some length in one of my recent books, *The Art of the Motor*.[3] A book is, admittedly, an instrument of memory. But, given the existence of the computer, of the dead memory disk, memory has clearly become a tool, a tool exploited by information technology. The question will arise tomorrow, then—and it will be a question of choosing or, at least, of 'sorting things out'—between live, living memory (that is to say, remembrance and life) and the dead memory of computer storage . . .

BRAUSCH. . . . This relates to the social bond and sociability, to the absence or presence of that sociability, as we said in one of our conversations prior to working on this book . . .

VIRILIO. To answer your question on living memory more precisely—I'm talking about human memory here, not machine memory—I'd like to say that this memory is the memory of the present.

That the acceleration we see now is no longer the acceleration of history, as heralded by Braudel or by the historians of the early twentieth century, but the acceleration of reality. When we speak of virtual reality and cyberspace, we're speaking of the acceleration of reality. When we speak of globalization rather than nationalization, we're speaking of the acceleration of reality. In a way, then, memory is accelerated. Memory, in its essence . . . And I'd remind you here that the existence of nations and of passports for crossing borders are recent inventions, linked to the onset of Modernity. Before that, people travelled with letters of recommendation, letters of credit: these things opened doors and created bonds . . .

BRAUSCH. Memory has become mechanized . . .

VIRILIO. Yes, today it's become electronic. This has nothing to do with the sedimentation of living memory, to which we'll return later when we speak of historical society and the family, for example. This acceleration of memory opens up an extraordinary field of questions. What is it to know everything at every moment, or to aspire to know everything at every moment? I don't think there's an answer to this yet. What I can say is that it's something that's beyond me, since I live in the present. But I'm sure that the acceleration of history has already given way to the acceleration of reality and that this brings memory back into question. History was the memory of the world. Now, accelerated reality will demand—is already demanding—another memory. A genuine memory, but a memory different from that of computer disks or CD-ROMs. A memory different from that of the book alone or the screen image alone. I can't say what this living memory of an accelerated present will be. All I know is that it has to be invented and constructed, and this is a matter for us all. But it's a question that has, as yet, no answer.

BRAUSCH. That being said, and without engaging in futurology, which in my view (professional futurologists will have to forgive me) is a bit like reading tarot cards or gazing into a crystal ball (acceleration is simply moving too fast), we shall always be caught up and overtaken by time. I think, as you say, one can live only in one's time, through one's thinking, one's—intellectual, sensory and corporeal—way of living and acting; that is to say, one can live only in the sense of being, of being in the world. History—and your history, which was so painful to evoke because you're a man of the real which is in the making and which you are making (and which we should all make, in fact, if we want to be conscious human beings)—history, then, as defined in dictionaries or the history of the last forty years, which was in large part the history of the Cold War, no longer exists. It's disappeared in the same way as ideologies have, which is itself a consequence of history's disappearance. This, I would argue, explains the importance of 'realist' philosophical thinking.

VIRILIO. To take forward what you're saying here, we have to pin down what accelerated reality might actually be. When we say 'acceleration of reality', the expression sounds good, but we have to try to pin it down, to circumscribe its meaning. It is, in fact, very simple and clear: it's real time.

BRAUSCH. History is real time.

VIRILIO. Yes. We used to live in a time that was an age of human beings and of the kind of memory I'd describe as physiological. Or of book-based memory, which is a slow, deferred memory. When you read, you're not synchronous with the event. The world is, however, beginning to live in synch with events as they take place. 'Real time' is winning out over the deferred time of direct memory, and of thinking too, with the reflex and the instant sensation gaining the upper hand. We're living 'live' now; we're no longer living the 'slowness' of the writer Milan Kundera. In this real time there is, then, a re-construction of memory to be undertaken. For the moment, sadly, we're a long way from achieving it. We have only the failings of the 'live'; we don't yet enjoy any of its benefits. This is what I wanted to say to pin down a bit more closely the effect of the acceleration of reality on our mode of life.

BRAUSCH. Where mode of life is concerned, I'd like to make a distinction between lived experience and knowledge, and knowledge through books—I take the book as an example of a primary didactic tool, but my question reaches as far as *savoir-vivre* and speaking and reading skills—though not in the sense of reading a crystal ball!

Where lived experience is concerned, it's definitely the case that the family has disappeared. It no longer exists in the sense in which history defined it from the dawn of time to the industrial—and even post-industrial—era. That means the balance between town and countryside disappears; this is a question that concerns both the territory and the nuclear family unit settled on the territory, whether in the countryside or in a town house. This 'lived experience' has disappeared from our age. Whereas the book, which is at first sight a dead object, begins—once it's been printed and distributed—to circulate, and you can come back to it as a source of individual liberty, verification, reflection and progress. I'd like to say right away that I understand the term 'progress' in the way it's defined by the young philosopher André Comte-Sponville in his *Le Mythe d'Icare: Traité du désespoir et de la béatitude*.[4] We have to stop vesting hope in linear progress, as passed down to us by history and the exact sciences, even into our post-industrial society. Sadly, we've not attended sufficiently, when it comes to living 'today', to the exponents of the fragment: Walter Benjamin, to name but one writer; Max Planck before the war; Benoît Mandelbrot and fractals since then. We should be 'wary' of the machine and regard it simply as a tool. Otherwise, we're back at the adoration of the Golden Calf! We should make use of the dead object (the book) as a sanctuary, in which memory is stored and sedimented, and 'dip into' it.

VIRILIO. These are answers that touch on my closest concerns and would call, therefore, for some very precise, if not indeed personal, questions and answers. I shan't, therefore, answer in that sense. What I can say, on the other hand, is that collective memory was linked to the nature of the unit of settlement: to the tribe, the village, the extended family as it still exists in Africa, the bourgeois family, and, most recently, the nuclear family, then the single-parent family and, today, the thoroughly individualistic family. It's true that in losing the demographic unit of settlement, we lose a collective memory and we necessarily fall back on the book—but not just any book: encyclopaedias, *Reader's Digests* and on what will replace—and is already replacing—the book: the CD-ROM or the computer disk, dead memory. I think you're right to say that memory involves men and women preserving a memory for their 'offspring', as we say. But that preservation has largely disappeared with the dissolution of the family. The invention of the book by Gutenberg corresponds to the state of the extended family. The disappearance of the book and the emergence of the CD-ROM corresponds to what's called the non-cohabiting couple. Here again, we've gone one step further than the single-parent family. This is the stage we've reached! The non-cohabiting couple isn't a family; it isn't even a couple, since the persons involved don't choose to live together.

BRAUSCH. It's a choice that jettisons responsibility in favour of shared diversions and pleasures that are forgotten as soon as they're consumed. This is so typical of our times . . . and we come back to the absence of bonds and sociability, and to our wish not to want (them) any more.

VIRILIO. I'd add that this situation arises out of the wear and tear of reality. Societies in the past lived slowly and put less strain on parental and marital relations.

BRAUSCH. There were also customary ways of behaving . . .

VIRILIO. Certainly. When we see the intensity and drama of a modern couple's life, the acceleration of reality has put a strain on what I would call the 'partners'. The term 'partner' indicates clearly that we aren't talking of a couple or a family here, but already of a game with reality in which each wears the other out . . .

BRAUSCH. Or the one uses the other and vice versa . . .

VIRILIO. Yes, and where the only future isn't pro-creation, but re-creation or, to give it its real name, divorce—i.e. the disappearance of 'being together'. Take Wim Wenders' film *Tokyo-Ga* and those millions of Japanese in the pachinko halls, hooked to their slot machines, totally hypnotized. Have you noticed that in cafes, alongside the notice saying 'Abuse of Alcohol is a Danger to Health', there's now one that says, 'The Abuse of Electronic Games can cause Epileptic Fits (the Management)'? At least in the former case individuals are free to choose whether to wreck their lives with alcohol, whereas in the latter the management is denying all responsibility for the danger to which it is, nonetheless, exposing the consumer . . . These are curious Tables of the Law!

BRAUSCH. It's here, as it seems to me, that the so-called exact sciences are directly at issue. We well know that Einstein bitterly regretted having discovered and disseminated the formula that made production of the atom bomb possible. I'd say that science today—and I'm thinking of a very specific example, here, since we're talking about the family: namely, artificial insemination—is operating at the limits and, consequently, forces a highly disciplinary ethics on us. I employ the term 'disciplinary' advisedly, because this kind of science is leading even more to solitariness, to pleasing 'oneself', to having a child 'for oneself', which is contrary to nature and love. You don't produce a child for yourself, but out of love and for the sake of the child itself. Or, to put it even more simply, out of the instinct—tempered today by reason and choice—to perpetuate life. Now, insemination is the other side of a process that's so natural, both for human beings and animals: namely, the perpetuation of the species—with the additional dimension of birth control and the control of sexuality in humans, of course.

VIRILIO. We can widen our thinking on this subject to all the biotechnologies: somewhere the awakening of the Golem—i.e. a creature manufactured completely from scratch—is being prepared. Indeed, it's already on the agenda. We're well aware that the 'value' of prostheses, not to say 'faith' in them, has grown to sizeable proportions. After xeno-transplantation—that is to say, organ transplants—we've reached techno-transplantation, as made possible by microcomputing. We're talking here of the nanotechnologies, the machines that can be transplanted into the body at a microscopic level.

BRAUSCH. You're reminding me of Ridley Scott's film *Blade Runner* and its subhuman types . . . the 'replicants'.

VIRILIO. Yes, it's an example of man's machine future—not a becoming-mechanical, which has already happened through conditioned reflexes— but a becoming-machine, which is now on the agenda . . . I wrote about this in my last book[5] and in *The Art of the Motor* and I think we're at the dawning of an invention here that's prefigured in the Golem myth. But it's a madness that will end in a great coming catastrophe, like the one that occurred fifty years ago. And it might, indeed, look like the fictional story of *Blade Runner*. They have enormous impact, these sciences that are no longer sciences of consciousness but of tyranny. And all in the name of a progress we now regard as sacrosanct, but which is uncontrollable and, inevitably, uncontrolled!

BRAUSCH. Hence the need, as I say, for an intensified ethics, though please understand that I'm not being negative or tyrannical (!) when I say that, but positive. This would be a complement to the Civil Code or the Human Rights Charter: the choice for life. Unfortunately, and here I've lost hope, though not in Comte-Sponville's sense—I really am in despair because we can do nothing about this—it's war between Man and Nature. Nature and humanity are engaged in a civil war. On this point, I'm with your philosopher friend Baudrillard: the ancestral survival instinct means that nature will always invent new diseases, new controlling 'plagues'—there's irony in this inversion—for the controlled survival of the species, which is a law of nature, even if the birth rate in the West has seriously plummeted. I'll give you a concrete example from the animal kingdom. To deal with rabies, they administered a treatment to vixens so that they would have litters of only one fox cub. But, in fact, the opposite happened: since nature and life were in danger, the vixens, which normally give birth to two cubs at the most—one or both of which may die by the natural process of selection—now had litters of six or seven cubs, to ensure the survival of the species . . . Immunology isn't a panacaea. I have to acknowledge a force of destiny here: the greater force of nature and life over humanity! And we can draw a parallel in this with technological viruses. We've been at war since the dawn of time and we shall be until the end. The great 'real' stakes of linear history—of life and death— have become fictive and fateful.

VIRILIO. We can come back, if you like, to geographical location and the social bond here, since

the place of settlement underpins the unit of settlement: if tribes were made up of hundreds of
persons, if extended families consisted of thirty
to fifty, that's because they lived on a territory
and roamed around it; they were not tied to one
restricted environment. The more the place of
settlement has become structured and developed,
through villages, towns, metropolises and mega-
lopolises or meta-cities, the more the unit of population—the family—has dissolved. We have
here a phenomenon of the unity of life, of the
demographic unity of human beings that's linked
to urbanism and architecture. Not to urbanism
in the sense of Le Corbusier's or any other
writer's theories, but to urbanism as a major historical and political phenomenon. The city, the
*polis* is, in my view, a major political phenomenon: the political form of history is the city.

BRAUSCH. Settlement . . . the place of settlement.
But I'd add, since we're in history here, that
when a port was involved—a place of departure
for the discovery of 'black holes'—it was all about

a policy of territorial conquest—and financial conquest too, the conquest of exotic commodities like spices and precious metals. All that was, however, quite natural and the ships were powered by the wind and ruled by *Chronos*. Today—we'll come back to this—the oceans are dead spaces where death-dealing cargo ships roam, ships carrying nuclear waste that no port will take.

VIRILIO. Of course. And you're right to speak of history, since these great adventures and their heroes are things of the past. The civil war you speak about between humanity and nature has the city as its battlefield today. That's the battlefield for this nature/culture opposition. The city's going through a transformation once again, after the industrial and post-industrial city, with the world-city and the megalopolis and the unit of global time that's replacing local time. We're on the eve of the globalization of the world. It isn't that cities will be built everywhere but that they will be synchronized. Demography and the species will become dependent on this temporal urbanism in new ways we can't yet imagine. We're currently at degree zero with non-cohabiting couples and I believe what's coming is even more astonishing than we think . . . and perhaps more catastrophic than we can imagine.

BRAUSCH. Once again I'm reminded of *Blade Runner*. There we're back in the dark ages, so to speak. We never see the sun on account of the pollution, which is already the case in Tokyo today. The skyscrapers, damaged by acid rain, are populated by people in survival mode. They're also the sites of civil war, of the resistance of sub-humans against their master—not unlike the *Commendatore* of Mozart's *Don Juan*—and they fight for love, the only feeling they're incapable of experiencing, that is to say, the thing that pre-vents them from procreating . . . Flying cars pass in the sky (Archigram had the same idea) and the 'normal' population (the white-collar workers) survive at ground level, like plague rats, sheltering under neon umbrellas that give them light and protect them from the unremitting acid rain. The only flourishing commerce is something like today's *Berliner Imbiss* (stalls selling Frankfurters and beer), Asian street bars where you can get a soup at any time of day or night . . . before going on your way without either fixed abode or social ties.

VIRILIO. If you like, this might be an opportunity to move on to terrain that you and I both know well: the city of the future and its architecture. Since the city and architecture are linked inextricably from this point on.

BRAUSCH. I think we can go on and speak about the city today, the problematic of emptiness and fullness, the continuum and the fragment, the local and the territory in time—in space-time—and, so far as space-time and globalization are concerned, I'd like to mention an entirely mundane—but real, not futuristic—example of our current mode of life in the city. A month ago, my brother, who's an international lawyer, found himself at his desk at five o'clock in the morning for a three-way Europe–US–Japan meeting—and I stress the word 'meeting'—for purposes of synchronicity . . . This is virtuality lived today in real time.

VIRILIO. This is obviously 'the' big question—and it's also the question of the definition of the local and the global. We don't realize how much global time—that single, universal time—conditions space. For the moment, your brother's 'timetable' is dependent on it, but tomorrow everyone's actions will be dependent on it, since, after all, we need the time to construct and organize space itself. Space will be dependent on global time, the way the building of a city like Prague or Paris was dependent on the local time of history. We can't yet know exactly how, but we can know that power relations will play their part in this, since history is, sadly, just one long struggle. Whether or not one's a peaceful individual, one can't help but be aware how much one needs resistance and a fighting spirit.

BRAUSCH. And imagination . . .

VIRILIO. . . . . Where that's concerned, I'd like to tell you something that struck me—and my friend the philosopher Edgar Morin—at a conference on global time, where I'd outlined the latest definition of the Pentagon's strategy for the US. Hold on tight, because this is an absolute historical inversion! From now on, the global, the globe—normally, a thing that encompasses the rest—is seen as the interior and the local is regarded as the exterior. In other words, we, who thought the pips were inside the apple, are outside the apple; we, who thought the quarters of the orange were inside the fruit, are, similarly, on the outside. You'll realize, as an urbanist, that this is a way of conceiving the local as the world's suburbs. The global—that is to say, real time, the power of immediacy, ubiquity, instantaneity—is the centre. And the whole of the local is the suburbs, the outside, the place of exile, the *out-land*.[6]

BRAUSCH. The *out of time*[7] too . . .

VIRILIO. This is a distinction that no one had dared conceive of before.

BRAUSCH. I'd almost say that it's a Copernican anti-revolution . . . and I use the term 'revolution' advisedly in the dual sense of time and war. And, I'd add that it's a revolution/volatilization.

VIRILIO. This raises a major question for us: How are we going to find a home for the virtual in the local? How are we going to build the architecture of the world-city if the centre is the global and the local is external? How are we going to build houses inside this world-city to put virtual space into them alongside the current spaces where people sleep, eat, wash and, in a word, live.

BRAUSCH. That's a vital question!

VIRILIO. A question of survival. How do we give the virtual a place in the actual?

BRAUSCH. I'm inclined to sum up your thinking by saying that there's currently a war between this black hole and the physiological functions of the human being . . .

VIRILIO. Yes.

BRAUSCH. We're in that black hole.

VIRILIO. Yes, but there are already people working on this question, albeit that they're trying to develop a virtual space that would complement the division into rooms, into spaces of the apartment or building, the tower block, etc.

BRAUSCH. We know some of them, who are indeed architects. There's Rem Koolhaas who was the first to point out that the empty space is of equivalent value to—or greater value than—the full. There's Jean Nouvel and his work, whatever some people think of it, on the form of the solitary object, whether transparent or otherwise. And there's the Japanese architect Toyo Ito, who, where there's 'nothing', invents a landscape, etc.

VIRILIO. As I see it, Nouvel's Fondation Cartier building on the Boulevard Raspail in Paris makes direct reference to the virtual. It is, of course, very classical—perhaps even too classical—but it has the merit of heralding the virtualization of space, using current materials. Nouvel has succeeded in creating something symptomatic of the virtual in built form. The virtualization of tomorrow's buildings can't be far away. It's a kind of materialist prophecy of the immaterial things that are to come.

BRAUSCH. We might also quote Herzog and de Meuron in Basle or others. What strikes me, in terms of geometry in the classical sense and perspective, is that these buildings you term virtual can be read both as two-dimensional and as self-mirroring structures. In other words, they can be seen as a series of mirrors simulating infinite repetition, and depth . . . They make me think of the last scene of Orson Welles' film, in which the main character is seen stretching off to infinity in a mirror. But with a single bullet the mirror smashes to pieces: there's the sound of the broken glass and the virtual is gone . . . there's nothing left, except an echo of what remains of it in our memories. Is this a way of passing through the mirror, like Alice in Wonderland? I don't think so. It is a trip into the land of terror, rather, . . . and of errors.

VIRILIO. With you, I say: 'memory'. You say 'materialist-immaterial', and I add: but not disappearance![8]

BRAUSCH. There will be no disappearance, ever, even if the black hole we're currently in is anything but a climbing wall that we can cling to! It quite simply *is*. It's for us to find it and work on it. Perhaps even to make it material?

VIRILIO. Yes. Here we're back with the acceleration of reality and, specifically, the acceleration of reality in architecture. I'd remind you that architecture, even if it doesn't last for ever, is a long-term affair. It's built slowly. And, even if it's a subterfuge that's a necessary precondition for creation, architects need to believe in the long term. And not now the long term of the building site, but the durability of their works—even if they last for only fifty years or, in other words, two generations, possible transformations included. Now, the acceleration of reality calls this notion of durability into question both physically and mentally. We know—we've spoken about this—that there was a lot of talk in the 1960s about flexibility. In that respect the Pompidou Centre is an example of an obvious failure, with its sliding walls, its rising and falling ceilings. We know this was a sort of parlour game among architects. But, on the positive side, the Pompidou Centre was already a symptom of the mobilization of architecture, with its way of keeping pace with the acceleration of the real. That acceleration has gone as far as it can today. It's no longer merely about sliding a wall around mechanically or electronically. We're speaking here of a synchronicity between a concrete, material building and actions taking place instantaneously elsewhere. Elsewhere in the world or at a place beyond the location of this particular building.

BRAUSCH. This is what I call the black hole.

VIRILIO. The black hole, yes. A question for which we can find no answer; we can only circle it, circumscribe it. The way I act in these circumstances is a little the way other primates do. When something worries you, you have to act like the Indians, until the thing's defined and you're less afraid of it. At that point, you can begin to defend yourself against it.

BRAUSCH. I'm going to come back to the Pompidou Centre, Beaubourg. And, simply from a pragmatic standpoint, I don't quite agree with you on this. The visions of the Russians, particularly Leonidov, the 'provocations' of the British Archigram group—and their serious investigations of movement, or those of the Italian Futurists on speed—are summed up in the Beaubourg Centre, which is, as I see it, the only utopian building ever built. The only playground for grown-ups in Paris! It is concretely positive. And the open platform is, after all, the most flexible of structures! We know , this from the theatre. And take the prime counter-example to Beaubourg, the Musée d'Orsay, which Gae Aulenti has structured as a host of inextricable circuits. To the point where you're so afraid of missing something that you feel obliged to visit every nook and cranny and see everything. Even some hopeless daubs. Because I'll take this opportunity to say that I'm in favour of 'education' by the best, not through 'knowing everything' and 'seeing everything'. Our brains are, fortunately, naturally selective, so as to save room for 'random access memory', for those things worth remembering on account of their genuine worth! And what I also like at Beaubourg, that great ocean liner, is that it's a platform for meeting and chatting; a space of rest, if not indeed of peace. At any rate, it's a meeting place and a shelter for many of Paris' marginal people, to whom we'll return later, I think. In that sense, with or without culture, Beaubourg is a success in my view. Though it's going to disappear (like the benches in the Metro, replaced by uncomfortable individual seats so that tramps can't lie on them), since they're going to restructure the plaza in front of the building and the forum on the ground floor for reasons of control obviously (totalitarian society isn't as far away as we think!), so you won't be able to gather there like tribes any more, recognizing each other as members, at a time when many people today have only this group identity, since individually they are subhumans, almost as in *Blade Runner*. Many people are going to lose their social connection, their sociability, as a result. I deplore this bitterly in a megalopolis like Paris, which is already hard

enough to live in, the minute you have the slight-
est little setback in your (still) relatively comfort-
able little life.

Beaubourg is, in my view, a haven of peace,
at the opposite extreme from the Forum des
Halles Metro/RER hub in the heart of Paris, into
which all the suburban access trains feed and
which is, inevitably, a place of gang warfare, on
account of the consumption—what you can't
buy you have to steal—and the drug dealers. And
the two are often linked: dealers and con-
sumers/thieves who, in the fullest sense of the
word, pay the price of drugs . . .

VIRILIO. There again, it's most important not to
run away from the problem. We have to refuse to
do that, and to defend ourselves, since it's a war
arena. At any rate, I agree with you here, the
Forum is a resounding failure, akin to a concentration camp, whereas the intention was that it
should be a place of fluidity.

BRAUSCH. As we were talking of 'circumscribing',
I'd like to mention the artist Richard Long, since

I have my own way of thinking, which is more poetic, less warlike, but no less sharp than yours (!) He walks in the desert. He draws circles or lines with his feet and piles up little heaps of pebbles with his hands until he's circumscribed spaces and traced out forms. He's an urbanist or an architect in his own way. Of course, this is preparatory work for a later gallery exercise, that later work being urban, rarefied and abstract, but at the same time real. I find this activity deeply moving, since it's both useless and brimful of meaning for anyone who knows how to see and feel Long's message. We're a thousand miles from the mechanistic globalization of the world. It's a globalization on the microscopic scale, on the scale of the exhaustion of a man's steps, in a universal, philosophical dimension that's much stronger than any electronic invention, any Internet or cyberspace network. At least, I see it that way. Through a real act, it attains to the purest virtuality—not mechanical, of course, but spiritual and in tune with the cosmos. What a happy man he must be to live the poetry which, in our case, has gone from our lives.

VIRILIO. I'll use this to bring us back to architecture—though with my feet on the floor, like Long! What I have to say runs, to some degree, in the same direction! It's the same sort of investigation. Since its origins, architecture has had the virtue of naming things that cover and protect us, but have another value. Doors, walls, windows, floors and fireplaces are much more than they appear to us as architectural elements. In this area, these too are signs of 'being-in-the-world': 'being-in-the-world' is situated and involves the threshold (and hence the crossing of the threshold) of the door. It also involves localization, the wall that is a materialization of localization, and the window that began as a door/window . . .

BRAUSCH. Yes, as it still is with the doors of certain farms today, or stable doors with the lower part fixed and the upper part opening . . .

VIRILIO. The window only emancipated itself at a very late stage, becoming solely a window, the door and the window thereby acquiring their reciprocal autonomy. And then there's the floor.

. . . I'd like to analyse the development of these architectonic elements with you: let's analyze the window. And I'll do this because in another sense it emancipated itself the first . . . Even if this seems bizarre, it isn't in contradiction, as we'll see, with what I've just said. The window is the hole in the wall (it's a former master glazier telling you this), a claustra, which had the advantage of allowing one to see, but not to pass, through it. The first doors are windows. In the hut, there's no window; there's a door and a fireplace. When the window was invented, in the first sense I've been talking about, it was something on a religious scale: the heavens were allowed in through the window and you were going to be able to see through it. It was an object of voyeurism. There is, then, an immaterial dimension to the window.

BRAUSCH. You put me in mind of Jacques Brel's song, 'Petit, ne vois-tu rien venir, il y a un homme qui passe' . . .⁹ It's 'the' site of waiting in time for the person who'll come or not come, an observation that I see as occurring through a hole in the wall, or a frame, since those looking are waiting for a possible quarry, armed with their rifles 'in case it's the enemy'. They're looking within a space bounded by a definite horizon, that's to say, as far as their eyes can see. And then there's the old 'Sister Anne . . .' line.[10] So the window enables you to wait for something, good or bad. It is, effectively, symbolic of 'being' or 'not-being' in relation to the 'other', enemy or friend!

VIRILIO. Exactly, and if I take a leap forward in time, the window is now no longer a framework or frame. With the invention of cinema and television, we no longer have the picture painted by the painter, in which we see the landscape—whether the artist is called Bonnard, Matisse, Cézanne or Vermeer van Delft—but the window is going to become the screen. I come back here, as it were, to the second definition—the claustra—and, with electronic surveillance, it becomes a real-time screen: the window becomes screen. We're used to this. There's electronic surveillance in every shop today and it's spreading more and more. We're used to it. But it's a 'theft' of our freedom, committed, so to speak, without our realizing it. It's a 'wholly unofficial' piece of progress. The screen-window, whether we know it or not, is a virtual window.

As for the floor, that medium of movement and of the storage of dead weights (foodstuffs, materials, etc.), it's set itself in motion. It's become travelator, elevator, goods lift and vehicle. We could describe a lorry as a rolling floor and a goods lift as an ascending and descending floor.

BRAUSCH. Koolhaas has made a very good analysis of this in relation to the elevators in New York skyscrapers in his book *Delirious New York*.[11] Thanks to this ascending and descending floor, the life of the city is vertical inside the skyscraper, which may not merely be a place of residence, but also a site of commerce, etc. This is what's happening in Paris' 'Chinatown', the tower blocks of the thirteenth arrondissement—and elsewhere, of course—where the various floors have restaurants on them, workshops, launderettes, massage parlours, dwellings, etc. We might almost imagine the city shifting from its 'natural horizontal state' to a 'vertical state': the Schuiten brothers, who produce graphic novels, have imagined this in several of their books, with passages linking one skyscraper to another. You could almost imagine living without setting foot on the ground!

VIRILIO. Yes, floors have effectively been 'automobilized' through the invention of the vertical street and the motorway. We might say that the two major routes are the vertical motorway of the skyscraper and the horizontal motorway for automobiles. It's *totale Mobilmachung*—total mobilization—as Jünger put it during the war.

BRAUSCH. All of this being linked, of course, to time, to space-time, to real and virtual movement—in lifts, for example, where you don't feel the movement. That's most unpleasant: you feel deprived of your choice of motion!

VIRILIO. And then, there's the gate or door (*la porte*). That's the big question.

BRAUSCH. From mythic times, it has provided resistance. The Greeks or the Romans, for example—not to mention medieval warriors—tried to break down the gates of a city with battering rams, reinforced—symbolically and practically—with metal tips . . .

VIRILIO. Yes. The gate or door is symbolic of the open and the closed. And what, today, is the virtualization of the door? Is such a thing possible? What's the difference between the virtualization of the window and that of the door? The floor wasn't virtualized, but mobilized. But the door or gate opens up an extremely vast field of questions, from the gateway to the enclosure of the primitive settlement, and on via the Middle Ages and the Renaissance, to the exit from the underground system at Les Halles in Paris, which is a good example of the pip being outside the fruit, for example. What lies hidden behind the virtual door?

BRAUSCH. The door/gate being the most important—and, I would say, the most philosophical—

architectonic element, since it concerns 'entering into' and 'exiting from', it also opens up an extremely vast field of reflection in space-time and in real—instantaneous—time. You exit from a stretch of motorway through a kind of gate. You enter an area of the city through the gateway of the subway system. In each case, whether entering or exiting, you pass through a gateway; this is a pass-*porte* event (a play on words that conveys a genuine meaning). One is always 'going towards' something, including the virtual. Through a real gate or door (*porte*).

In this connection, I'd like to mention our friend the Berlin architect Daniel Libeskind, who recently told me a sort of parable. He asked me first what it meant to me to pass through a doorway of a house—which he saw as a basket to be filled up—carrying another basket filled with victuals, 'to take to someone in that house'. I naturally replied that it meant crossing the threshold. He gave me a shrewd look and asked, 'What if the door remained closed? What's the basket and what the victuals?' His answer, in the end, was that it wasn't the building that was the basket. The building itself was merely an outer shell and it was the person-to-person relation 'through' the door that was actually the basket and the victuals! Open, Sesame . . . door, open thyself . . . on to the memory of Berlin, including Nazi Berlin: don't close the door, the container of the content; the container of the symbolic 'power' of saying and doing! It was, indeed, for this reason that Libeskind, a Jew born in Poland in 1945 and raised in the US, came back to Berlin: he doesn't want the Jewish question to be 'ghettoized' into the 'accidental' chapter of the Nazi period; he wants it to be cosmopolitanized, to be amalgamated into the history of all Germans, as was the case before the war—in particular in Berlin, the cosmopolitan city par excellence.

VIRILIO. To come back more precisely to the door, let me add that Duchamp answered this question in a very simple way. In the knowledge that Duchamp is a genuine philosopher—philosophy can be painted or filmed, you don't have to write books. He actually invented a door that is both open and closed; a door at a corner. When it's open on one side, it's closed on the other and vice versa. I think that the 'Call Room', the simulator into which I welcome my (virtual) visitor, is, in a way, a door that's open, on condition that the other doors are closed! This brings us back to Duchamp's dialectic: the real door is either closed or open and there's no doubt about it; it's only by a 'mechanical' trick that you can say it's both open and closed. On the other hand, with the coming of the second, 'virtual' door—the door of the 'Call Room', of the virtual vestibule where the clone of my tele-visitor will appear—my apartment will actually be closed so far as the real door goes but virtually open where the simulator of the presence of my spectral guest is concerned.

BRAUSCH. So, the way he puts it, Libeskind's definition is exactly right . . .

VIRILIO. Absolutely. And so is Duchamp's: doors today are both open and closed. We have, for example, all the woes of the world streaming out at us through the television, but we're not aware of the plight of our neighbour, who may, in fact, be in danger next door. Do you remember the advert for *Médecins du Monde* that showed a woman peacefully ensconced in her flat with her children? She's been watching the horrors of Rwanda on television. Suddenly, the door to her apartment opens and you see a skeletal individual really walk in—a Rwandan child. Naturally, the woman reacts anxiously, indicating that the family had become habituated to the virtual presence of unfortunate children dying of starvation or being massacred at the ends of the Earth. But when this little unfortunate came through the real door, the effect was frightening. This well demonstrates that these two doors function in opposite ways.

BRAUSCH. I had big discussions with my family on this subject when Jacques Lanzmann's film *Shoah* was broadcast on television. This was, I suppose, an act of rebellion on my part, a provocative act too, since I didn't live through the wartime persecution, but I try, nonetheless, to live with awareness—I might almost say, on my guard—in our own times. Of course, my family found Lanzmann's film very disturbing, having themselves been on the good side (it's horrible to put it this way, since, in that period, this meant being on the victims' side). And part of my family experienced betrayal and deportation. But I asked them: What would you do today if the Senegalese street cleaner was attacked? What would you say if I brought home a black or Arab boyfriend? Do you have the political consciousness that's needed today—particularly at neighbourhood level? Would you be active? Would you 'act'?

VIRILIO. That's just it . . . One of these doors, the real one, the house door, receives and welcomes, whereas the other, the television, habituates us to not welcoming. Instantaneous news coverage is a tragedy of this century's end. We experience it passively; it prevents us from being aware of the things going on around us; this brings us back to the problematic of place and social bonds.

BRAUSCH. In the precise case of this example, the virtual is more real than the real and vice versa. It's an anecdotal, micro-scale example, but we have to be aware that the same phenomenon is occurring at the macro-level—the planetary, philosophical, symbolic level. We need only think of the Trojan Horse in Greek mythology! And we're always arriving at and returning from a space. What is the space beyond the door, beyond the threshold?

VIRILIO. Twelve years ago I published *L'Espace Critique*,[12] in which I said that the notion of the 'critical' no longer applied simply to situations or to moments in time (the moment before leaping into the void, for example), but to the very notion of space. That was in 1984. Now it so happens that it was also in 1984 that *Neuromancer* was published, the book in which William Gibson first used the word 'cyberspace'.[13] I'd say that virtual space is a realization of critical space, the critical space I spoke of as taking the form of fractals and deconstructive geometry. I'd remind you that fractals are deconstructed geometry: it isn't architecture that's deconstructed but geometry itself. The appearance of fractal geometry in Mandelbrot's work will call into question the whole character of space, which was the basis of the work of architects and, I'd contend, of all those who work 'in the field'.

BRAUSCH. So, the three-dimensional is called into question, in favour of two-dimensionality and the embedded spiral . . .

VIRILIO. Virtual space will set critical space 'in action' through the crisis of real space, the crisis we've just spoken about. Real space is less important than real time and this critical space will have to be built with a new architecture, a new architectural thinking—an entirely different way of perceiving space-time from what we've been used to between the Quattrocento, with its perspective, and now. I think it's important to realize that, after seeing ethics enter into crisis, followed by politics and ideologies, this century's end is seeing a crisis in the notion of aesthetic spatiality. Not just geometric spatiality—whole and fractional dimensions—but the space of reality experienced by millions of people in their cities and homes. So cyberspace isn't the technical wizardry of the CD-ROM, which is just an on-screen electronic dictionary, or simulator gadgetry that can frighten or entertain. It's real space coming into crisis. Critical space is becoming a contemporary phenomenon in individuals' lives.

BRAUSCH. And critical is meant in the sense of alarm . . .

VIRILIO. Of course! In the sense that we can no longer trust space. Euclidean space is no longer a credible space. Nor is the space of topology, because the topological character of oriented surfaces is now topped by fractal geometry: we're in another space. The architect has to work with this space in crisis. Hence deconstruction. But the question is: How far can it go? How far can deconstruction go?

BRAUSCH. I know you're thinking of Libeskind, the Coop Himmelb(l)au group and others. I'd add the Japanese architect Toyo Ito, who's patiently deconstructed the geometric constituents of architecture, one by one, to arrive at working with 'reticulated' spaces, landscaped territories. Even when there's nothing there, he creates a landscape into which he sets his architecture and he works on the light, of course. He began with a totally closed space, the U-shaped house, where only the light brushing the walls created the space, and he arrived at his own house—which is a  built cyberspace, in which each necessary (otherwise it would no longer be architecture) element scrambles the reading of the others—at the Wind Tower at Yokohama, an air-conditioning tower for a car park, concealed by several layers of metal cladding, where several sets of artificial lights, operating to different rhythms, respond to the intensity of noise, the degree of pollution, etc. He's the one who's gone furthest along this path.

VIRILIO. Yes, I know. And the fluid territory of the city.

BRAUSCH. Perhaps deconstructed architecture means flows? But, all the same, I'd make a clear distinction—this is a little 'aside'—between the notion of deconstructivism in philosophy and deconstructivism in the field of architecture, which, I say again, is necessarily something constructed. Architecture will always mean building something. Hence, in fact, the difficulty of putting a name to this deconstruction, which is, on the face of it, at odds with the very business of the architect . . . And I see a parallel here with our two-speed society with, on the one hand, the globalization of the pips spinning round the outside of the globe/fruit and the satellite technology that is the preserve of those who will have access to the 'Call Room', and, on the other hand, the world of those who live with their feet on the ground—not, sadly, in Long's sense—but in the street, when they are outside, and in front of their televisions, when they are at home and passively taking in virtual events and the lies and virtual manipulations of the media and politicians. For they won't perhaps have the good fortune of seeing the door open and the little Rwandan walk in . . . So our age is a time of *Star Wars* within the space of our planetary experience and of civil war back down on the terra firma of our 'hearths and homes', as we say in sensible, down-to-earth language! And then there's worse. And you know this because you've worked on this problem. For those who are already adrift or down and out, there's what we might call the 'mean streets'. This is the most realistic stage of the real city!

VIRILIO. This issue is obviously close to my heart in the form of what are called the 'homeless': those people of 'no fixed abode' who are, as it happens, another illustration of the non-cohabiting couple. I'd like to say that the homeless are an expression, at the level of political society, of what the non-cohabiting couple represents within the family and the unit of settlement. We're in the same two-speed logic, even if the examples are different.

BRAUSCH. I'd like to say three-speed or two-and-a-half-speed, since 'Mr and Mrs Average' sitting in front of their TV lies aren't 'conscious'. Fortunately not, as my mother says: otherwise, there'd be a revolution! My answer is always that we—and that includes these 'zombies'—are living through a civil war. Perhaps the worst one ever, except for the Terror during the French Revolution, which was a time of great bloodshed. But the clean civil war we're living through today is all the more pernicious . . .

VIRILIO. Let's stick with two speeds, since that's generally accepted. There are those who spend most of their time in the real time of teleworking, share prices and the globalization of an abstract reality, and there are those who have no access to these things and live off-the-pace in the 'deferred' time of manual labour (production workers, labourers, etc.). The first society lives in real time and at the centre of things by the inverted Pentagon definition I mentioned a moment ago, whereas the second society lives in 'deferred' time, outside, in the global suburbs, in that periphery where local time is dominated by global time.

BRAUSCH. They have themselves become satellites, while the first society makes use of satellite technology . . .

VIRILIO. In today's cities, two different temporalities are set against each other. But those who live in real time are few in number—even if there are already millions of people wired up to the Internet—whereas those living in deferred time can be counted in billions! We can see the degree to which the town/country opposition is changing for a last time. Town/country was the nineteenth-century opposition. Before the nineteenth century, there was no town/country opposition, since the towns lived off the produce of their rural hinterlands. From the Industrial Revolution onwards, towns and cities stood in opposition to the countryside, leading to the transformation of the peasantry into a proletariat.

BRAUSCH. And that was seen as progress, since the industrial era is the age of progress. Except that they weren't yet aware that there's no progress without collateral damage—without losers!

VIRILIO. From the twentieth century onwards, we have the urban/suburban opposition. The opposition shrinks in spatial terms. We're not talking now about sucking people and goods in from a whole national territory, but about a commuter lifestyle: working in the city and sleeping in the suburb. In France, the suburbs would soon be abandoned to their fate. An illustration of this is the signing of the Charter on 25 May 1996 of the thirty-four so-called 'free zones', in an attempt to lift these critical areas out of their state of financial collapse. Last comes the twenty-first century—and we're already living in it[14]—with the opposition between the settled and the nomadic. In other words, between those who are adrift and not, any longer, in the hinterland, the 'land behind' or the 'backward' part of town, but in the *out-land*,[15] looking for short-term employment contracts of a

few months at best, and hoping those contracts
will perhaps be renewable . . .

BRAUSCH. Or for something to hang on to physically and mentally to survive—or, if there were
such a word, to 'sub-vive' . . .

VIRILIO. Yes. I might mention a woman who's
currently in this position, who told me, 'Looking
for a part-time job is a full-time job' . . .

BRAUSCH. Not so long ago, when I was a journalist on *Le Moniteur* (a weekly magazine that I
left in 1989), I remember we were all dreaming of
having modems, so we could live in the country
and be linked electronically to terminals in the
city. And I particularly remember a competition
run by the PAN (new architecture) programme
of the Ministry of Infrastructure and Territorial
Development, the theme of which was 'A Habitat for Nomads'. But this was meant in a positive
sense, as progress. The idea was that, thanks to
planes, high-speed trains and generally shorter
journey times, freely available, super-efficient
workplaces, spread, more or less, around every

town and city, would enable us to work in better tele-working conditions using mobile phones and portable computers. The aim was to invent a new 'habitat' for these new nomads, permanently in transit but comfortably so. There was even excitement about these new buildings that looked a bit like student residences and had a rediscovered tribal conviviality. But to see things like this was a luxury. The Gulf War, the wars in Yugoslavia and Africa, the bankruptcy of the Western states, the opening of the Berlin Wall (even if that was an important human event at the economic level, it's catastrophic for Germany and the whole of Europe, which hasn't taken sufficient responsibility for the former Soviet Bloc countries) and, later, helping to create a Palestinian state alongside Israel, which has to be sustained at all costs, humanitarianly and economically, have all thrown a spanner in the works of this fine 'humanized, machinized' future vision.

VIRILIO. The woman I mentioned, a former secretary to the Interdepartmental Urban Commission

. . . is a mere typist today, on the verge of sliding into long-term unemployment. Her comment is worth repeating: 'Looking for a part-time job is a full-time job' . . .

BRAUSCH. I'll add to what you're saying by turning to a theme I can't talk about enough at the moment: the 'politically correct'. No one talks about this and yet it's the real modern illustration of Goethe's colour theory: mix up all the primary colours you like—red, yellow, blue, etc.—and the result you get will be grey. We're grey mice—and forced to be so! And this is a problem at several levels. It's a problem at the level of reality for 'white-collar' workers in Japan, for example, who are absolute robots and are forced, in the evenings, to go and get drunk on sake with their bosses, in the company of geishas, the symbols of 'feminine companionship'. We're back again with the non-cohabiting couples, since often, because the Tokyo suburbs where these robots live are so immense, they sleep in cell-like single-person hotels, over-provided with electronic gadgets, located near the subway stations that will take them back to their slavish occupations the next day . . .

And then—and here I'm onto a subject which we sadly shan't be able to discuss sufficiently: namely, the advance of science and one of its consequences, the longevity of human beings—a family is now frequently made up of four generations. But what are we to do with the old people who, in the days of the life in the 'hinterland' of the countryside, looked after the children while the parents were in the fields. What are we to do with them except 'leave it to society to look after them', the flats we live in being too small? We put them in asylums we euphemistically term 'old people's homes' . . . And even if someone has every educational qualification going, like your secretary friend, how will our children have to live, what price will they have to pay to look after us in retirement? At forty-five years of age, society wants nothing more to do with us . . . Beyond a certain age, society takes our responsibilities from us and throws us away like a worn-out object.

VIRILIO. This might be the point, if you like, to talk about the *balise de survie* project,[16] which we mounted, as teachers, with the students of the École spéciale d'architecture in Paris and then expanded, with Chilpéric de Boiscuillé, into an international competition. The *balise* was a kind of lifeboat on the urban sea, a building providing minimum services to people who were struggling but not yet down-and-out. It had facilities for washing and for washing clothes, 'luggage lockers' for storing a few possessions and documents, and the necessary technical equipment— a television to keep up with the news, computers to print a CV on, Minitels, etc. We were shamelessly derided and attacked by 'politically correct' society. Selfishly, society wouldn't face up to the real facts of the situation. People don't mind giving a few coins to a poor person in the street, who is often flanked by one or more dogs who are their companions both for emotional warmth and for defence against being robbed while they're sleeping on the streets . . . I'm not talking about the tramps of Paris—*les clochards*—who are pretty much an element of folklore, though you hardly see any of them today. This game of the 'spectre of misfortune' is a very real game, in which society is playing with people's lives and has the power of life and death over thousands of them. Well, it doesn't want them to survive. These aren't concentration camps, but as soon as you 'slide' on to the streets, you're done for. You're as good as dead. You're civically, individually dead . . . The social bond is broken.

BRAUSCH. It was a project dealing with a genuine emergency and I was, in fact, sickened by the way you were violently attacked over it. I wrote to *Le Monde* after they published a scandalous, disgusting article about it, which flatly denied that the problem existed. Even *Le Monde*, which has a reputation as a serious, 'free' newspaper, didn't publish my letter.

VIRILIO. Politically correct society is criminally in denial: it denies the state of civil crisis we're experiencing as a result of the changes in the modes of production and circulation. Every time there's a change in the mode of production, things go badly. We're moving from an industrial, if not indeed post-industrial, mode—we went through its battles in the 1970s with the two oil crises—to an information-based mode of production, through automation, hyper-productivity, etc. There'll be a period of adaptation that will take some time, during which substantial harm will be incurred. We know what dramas ensued from the shift from an agrarian to an industrial mode. The works of Dickens or Zola are there to show us. We must be under no illusion today. The trauma caused by this change will go on for one or two generations before we find new rules for the economy and new rules of social justice. It's impossible to be more precise than that. Those who say 'It's just a passing crisis and everything will work out' are not only liars but, as you say, also criminally in denial.

BRAUSCH. Demagogues . . .

VIRILIO. . . . And they're the ones who get in the

way of the difficult work done by social workers, sociologists, doctors and people of good will in general. For very real reasons, our politicians have time to make the fullest use of the media. Their aim is to get elected and re-elected; that's the issue for them, that's what the political 'game' is about. But you'd think they'd forgotten what it means to represent citizens and their desires and grievances . . . And here I come back to our discussion or, rather, to our realization that there's a civil war on. Apart from the 'subhumans' of the street—and their dogs—that we've just talked about, we're back to a kind of clan warfare between little drug barons and other kinds of medieval figures, all peddling their—destructive—products, like the freely available guns we see in the US. So clan warfare is back in our cities. I'd remind you that we're no longer seeing continents consigned to Third World status, as occurred in Africa or Asia half a century ago, but cities themselves, be it in the US, Europe or elsewhere . . . So far as the availability of guns is concerned, and to come back here to the question of the—closed or open—door, I think that if the majority of people sitting in front of—and morbidly enjoying—the images of the world's catastrophes parading across their TV screens were confronted with the spectre of the little Rwandan, they would prefer to gun him down on their doorstep!

BRAUSCH. This situation of the city's decomposition into clans, mafias and internecine warfare between individuals, which you've just mentioned, is one of the elements of urban deconstruction. It's happening in the biggest cities. In Washington, for example, young people are under a 'curfew'! It's clear that the question we analysed of geometric deconstruction, familial or architectural deconstruction, is all reflected in the deconstruction of the city and the social deconstruction we're calling 'civil war'. Even if it's a virtual civil war, it's a very real producer of the living dead—through unemployment, the collapse of support mechanisms and individuals being set adrift.

This is chaos' knock-out blow.[17] It's due in large part—perhaps I'm repeating myself, but I don't understand why the majority of people aren't aware of this—to the belief in a progress that will always bring well-being and a better life . . . I'll come back here to the problem of excessive immunology and a nature that will always invent 'regulative' plagues and illnesses. We can't do anything about that and never will be able to . . . Excessive belief in progress and science is also a sort of revisionism. One hopes in a way that's almost physiological, whereas one should know that there's only an *entre-deux* between the beginning—coming into the world—and the end—death. And that *entre-deux* is life on Earth. For me, this is the big problem. It's the question of relativism that you talked about in one of our earlier interviews.

VIRILIO. I don't think we can go any further on this. Let's come now to the last part of our conversations. Here I would say, in conclusion, not, like Nietzsche, that 'God is dead', but that in the place of the God of monotheism, Judaism and Christianity we have elevated a machine god, a *deus ex machina*, and today's atheists are merely the devotees of the cybernetic machine god, the god of prostheses, etc. There's a fundamentalism of science and technology, just as there's a mystical fundamentalism. So, to come back to the progress you were just mentioning, there's no gain without a loss. When the elevator is invented, we lose the staircase. Of course there is still a staircase, but it becomes an emergency exit. When we invent the supersonic plane, we lose the ocean liner and the ocean liners become cargo ships, dustbins wandering around on dead seas, leading one day, perhaps, to some great catastrophe.

BRAUSCH. But they become also—to strike an optimistic note—rescue ships, like the survival units for the homeless.

VIRILIO. To stay with the topic of space and city planning, there's an element I'd like to discuss and that's grey ecology. I think this might be of relevance to a lot of readers. Unlike in France, ecology in Germany is a very important element and a political instrument. Now, the ecology in question is an ecology of nature; the German ecologists, the *Grüne*, are opposed to the pollution of substances that make up Nature. You've just talked about this, in a way, in speaking of the nuclear waste ships. But alongside the ecology of the pollution of Nature, there's the ecology of the pollution of what French calls *la grandeur-nature*, which means life-size, the scale of life. This latter ecology is an ecology of distances; it's what I call grey ecology. The distances between things are a part of Nature. Putting things together or separating them is part of Nature, and distances are part of substances. Now, all the progress made in acceleration—both of history and of reality (after the transport and communications revolutions)—merely reduces distances to zero. First material, terrestrial distances, through railways, motorways and air travel: then immaterial, electromagnetic distances, through the invention of telecommunications. There is, then, a great threat on the horizon.

The threat Foucault locates in the eighteenth century, the ideology of the 'great confinement', in fact lies ahead of us. The confinement Foucault speaks of is the confinement of the mad in asylums, but what's coming down the track for us is the confinement of human beings on a planet reduced to nothing. And a sense of imprisonment will develop—is already developing—in a society where travel is no longer a formative experience for young people, because they've already—through the media—seen the world and 'travelled' around it from earliest childhood. I believe that, for the people of *Wanderung*, for the peoples of romantic Europe, there's an enormous threat here, which I feel represents an exhaustion of the world as a body extended in space and time . . .

BRAUSCH. I come back to the quotation from Deleuze about Beckett that was the epigraph to the first interview in this book. It's something Léo Ferré said in his own way, 'There's nothing more, nothing nothing more.' But we aren't exhausted!

VIRILIO. Immaterial pollution can't be seen. Or, rather, it can be seen on television. The pollution of a world reduced to nothing, a world you can travel round as we travel round a city, in no time at all, using hypersonic planes that will take just two hours to get to Tokyo—the time it takes to get from Paris to Lyon on today's high-speed train—or tele-conferencing and interactive technology that will bring all the world's cities together in the 'Call Room'. I believe this interactivity the cyberneticists so desire is an end of the world. Not in an apocalyptic sense, but it's a reduction of the world, a sort of a death and destruction of the world as life-size entity.

BRAUSCH. Hence the importance in my view— and this is also one of those questions that troubles me constantly, both as architect and teacher—of understanding emptiness, the empty space. We know that so-called avant-garde architects, who are simply the good architects of our present age, have understood that empty space is of equivalent significance to full space, and know how to work on it in the same way. They became aware some ten or even fifteen years ago of its equal importance; aware of the meaning of empty space . . . and the fact that we need it! . . .

VIRILIO. Of the meaning of anti-form . . .

BRAUSCH. In relation to three-dimensional space . . . Of 'open spaces' in the traditional sense, of intervals in the musical sense, in the territorial sense, to speak symbolically of distance, and in the global sense. I would even add: in the sidereal sense of the position of our planet in its galaxy and of that galaxy in the Great All that makes up the world. The majority of people just will not understand, because if you say 'emptiness', they take it to mean loss. Loss of sense, as in an attack of dizziness. Only a small elite of thinkers and 'makers' accept it—among them a number of architects.

VIRILIO. With this notion of interval, of emptiness and fullness, we touch on something that's always been fundamental to my work: work on speed. I believe today that the economics of speed is as indispensable as the economics of wealth. The only art in which there's an economics of speed is music. Until we have a musical economics of speed in society, we shan't have resolved the question of the acceleration of present reality (*l'accélération de l'actualité*).

BRAUSCH. Absolutely, in the musical sense it's entirely natural, since what is music but rhythm? A minim, a crotchet, a quaver, a semi-quaver, a rest; *forte*, *fortissimo*, *allegretto* . . . the conscious manipulation of time. There's a whole spectrum of nuances . . .

VIRILIO. *Allegro ma non troppo . . . molto vivace*! The acceleration of reality requires a music of reality or, in other words, a composition of speeds that's on a par with musical composition.

BRAUSCH. The problem is that, of all the arts, music is the most abstract, the most virtual. Sound is perceptible only by the sense of hearing. The problem, to come back to our profession as architects, urbanists, architecture critics, etc., is that ours is an art of the real and is, of all the arts, the one most concerned with constructing the world!

VIRILIO. In my view, by way of the oblique function and the deconstruction of architectural geometry, we have to move from music to choreography!

BRAUSCH. . . .Which is movement. How should we move? This is probably the question of the future, since it involves a relation both to the reality of physical behaviour over long distances and to the virtuality of still—in the sense of 'concentrated'—thought.

So, in conclusion, I come back to your first question: 'Is the origin the end (*la fin*)?' and to my play on words: 'And is it also hunger (*la faim*)?'

VIRILIO. Kafka said: 'I cannot live without writing in order to understand . . .'

BRAUSCH. And we know what prophetic things he wrote about the eternal reality of the human condition! This is a conclusion for us, driven as we are by curiosity, for us walkers in the city, like

Perec and others—Debord, Restif de la Bretonne, Poe, Canetti . . . Sadly, we haven't broached the problem of the enthusiasm and fear of crowds, but that will be for another day!

I'd like to conclude with the question of 'virtual being': you're a believer and I'm a non-believer. What I have learned, ultimately, through these four interviews is summed up for me in the last words of your tribute to Müller: '*Adieu, à Dieu.*' This brings us back to our condition as thinking and sentient human beings, and to the ether. And to peace perhaps?

In conclusion, let me complement your quotation from Kafka, if you don't mind, with some lines on real time from a poet/singer of my generation, Bernard Lavilliers: 'Ahead of us the year 2000, just a few steps away. Don't speak of it, I've been told. Yet that silence has something of an accursèd swing that sets the clocks aright . . .'[18]

*Notes*

1  In French, *la fin* and *la faim* are homophones.—
   Trans.

2  Jorge Semprun and Élie Wiesel, *Se taire est
   impossible* (Paris: Mille et une nuits, 1997).

3  Paul Virilio, *L'Art du moteur* (Paris: Galilée,
   1993); *The Art of the Motor* (Julie Rose trans.)
   (Minneapolis: University of Minnesota Press,
   1995).

4  André Comte-Sponville, *Le Mythe d'Icare: Traité
   du désespoir et de la béatitude* (Paris: PUF, 1984).

5  The reference is presumably to *Un paysage
   d'événements* (Paris: Galilée, 1996); *A Landscape
   of Events* (Cambridge: The MIT Press, 2000).

6  In English in the original.—Trans.

7  In English in the original.—Trans.

8  It is, in fact, Virilio who appears to have introduced
   the 'materialist-immaterial' idea. The discrepancy
   most probably arises as a result of the original editing of the dialogue for the French edition.—Trans.

9  Literally, 'Boy, don't you see anything coming?
   There's a man going by . . .'—Trans.

10 The reference is to Charles Perrault's 'Bluebeard'
   and, in particular, to the line, 'Sister Anne, do
   you see someone coming?'—Trans.

11 Rem Koolhaas, *Delirious New York: A Retroactive Manifesto for Manhattan* (New York: Monacelli Press, 1978).

12 Paul Virilio, *L'Espace critique* (Paris: Christian Bourgois, 1984); *Lost Dimension* (New York: Semiotext(e), 1991).—Trans.

13 William Gibson, *Neuromancer* (New York: Ace Books, 1984).

14 It should be remembered that these conversations were first published in 1997.—Trans.

15 In English in the original.—Trans.

16 A project for the design and production of a sort of 'survival station' for struggling urban 'nomads' which developed largely into a project to assist the homeless.—Trans.

17 There is a pun here on the homophones '*le K.O.*' and '*le chaos*'.—Trans.

18 This is my own translation of Lavilliers' lines, as cited from memory (with two minor errors) by Marianne Brausch. Lavilliers plays on the expression '*mettre les pendules à l'heure*', which means, literally, to set clocks to the right time and, figuratively, to set the record straight.—Trans.